The Spelling List and Word Study Resource Book

Greek and Latin roots, word histories, organized spelling lists, and other resources for dynamic vocabulary and spelling instruction

By Mary Jo Fresch and Aileen Wheaton

SCHOLASTIC
Teaching
Resources

NEW YORK · TORONTO · LONDON · AUCKLAND · SYDNEY
MEXICO CITY · NEW DELHI · HONG KONG · BUENOS AIRES

Dedication

To our husbands,
Hank and Jim

Love seems the swiftest, but it is the slowest of all growths.
No man or woman really knows what perfect love is until
they have been married a quarter of a century.
—Mark Twain's Notebook

Cover design concept by Vito Zarkovic
Cover design by Maria Lilja
Interior design by LDL Designs
Cover photos: top left and right by Mary Jo Fresch; bottom left © The Image Bank/Getty Images;
top center © Corbis; bottom right © Photo Disc/Getty Images
Interior photos by Mary Jo Fresch
Map on page 12 by James McMahon

ISBN 0-439-44407-1
Copyright © 2004 by Mary Jo Fresch and Aileen Wheaton
All rights reserved. Published by Scholastic Inc.
Printed in the U.S.A.
3 4 5 6 7 8 9 10   23   09 08 07 06 05 04

Contents

Acknowledgments

Words are powerful tools. Words can encourage, inspire, affirm, challenge, and create curiosity. This book is a result of encouragement, inspiration, and affirmation bestowed to us by those of greatest influence in our lives. Many have guided and supported us throughout this journey. Our greatest companions are our beloved children and husbands. And last, we thank the many students that have passed through the doors of our classrooms; they became *our* teachers in many ways.

One thing life has taught me: if you are interested, you never have to look for new interests.
They come to you. When you are genuinely interested in one thing,
it will always lead to something else.
—Eleanor Roosevelt

Foreword

Mary Jo Fresch and Aileen Wheaton speak directly to teachers in this practical resource that will be a very valuable addition to a teacher's professional library. *The Spelling List and Word Study Resource Book* addresses an important area related to competent literacy—knowledge of words, their structure and meaning. Understanding of words allows readers and writers to behave in highly strategic ways, making word solving efficient as well as effective. This competency is so important because it frees attention for the goal of reading and writing—comprehension and composition of written text.

The authors have connected word structure and word meaning in ways that contribute to decoding and spelling skills as well as to the expansion of vocabulary and, ultimately, comprehending abilities. Their view of "word study" goes well beyond spelling to encompass a wide scope of knowledge, to include word origins and histories and connections between and among larger categories of words.

As competent readers and writers, much of our own knowledge of words is at an implicit level. We may know how to inflect a verb, understand the meaning of a prefix, or automatically double a consonant when adding an ending but be unable to cite the explicit "rule" of the language that tells us to do so. It just seems to "sound right" or "look right" and we keep our attention on the meaning of the text that we are reading or writing. Nevertheless, the fundamental knowledge is there and it underlies our ability to read and write with a high level of skill.

As teachers, we want to be sure that our students' experience with words is as rich as possible so that they, too, build such a foundation of understanding. It is useful to call this knowledge to mind in an organized way when planning lessons. This book will help you achieve that goal. In it you will find an interesting and readable account of language that will be enlightening and serve as a resource for your teaching. You will enjoy the word roots and histories, ponder intriguing types of words, and explore idioms and their origins. Most helpful will be the organized word lists that give you instant examples for the lessons you are teaching daily and that are helping children learn how words "work."

—Gay Su Pinnell, Ohio State University

Introduction

By words the mind is winged.
—Aristophanes (450 BCE–385 BCE)

Words are power. Think of the intensity and intent in words such as "I have a dream," "Four score and seven years ago," and "ask not what your country can do for you, ask what you can do for your country." As educators, we are entrusted to hand down language's power to our students—a rich cadre of words and also an appreciation of the historical legacy of our English language imparted to us by various cultures of the world. We want students to be fascinated by language's continual evolution and to notice how words change meaning over time as they are defined and redefined by different speakers and cultures. This is what this book is about.

Once we begin to explore words and their histories with our students, we appreciate that the English language is more predictable than we were once led to believe. Does this mean you and your students should research every word you encounter in your reading and writing? No. But we do believe you need a curiosity that guides language learning in your classroom. Teachers need not be "word masters," but need to share their joy of an on-going journey of discovery about the language. That's why we embrace the term "word study." "Spelling" simply refers to the conventional reproduction of a word in print. "Word study" encompasses the notion of exploring word origins, histories, meanings and relationships between words. Spelling is a part of word study, but word study should not simply be spelling.

The purpose of this book

There are many resources that contain graded spelling lists, word histories, word stories and information about the evolution of common words. All of these resources, both print and electronic, can help support a good word study program for students. However, busy teachers find that searching through a multitude of resources and selecting appropriate words for spelling and word study is time consuming. Therefore, it is our desire that this book will provide both spelling and word study resources in one handy place. We hope you will "dip" into this book often throughout the school year. Look for connections between topics and themes you currently teach and the stories about words shared here.

You will notice the spelling word lists in this book contain carefully selected words reflecting developmentally appropriate features for students to study. So why did we choose these features and these words? We like to think of literacy instruction as "dancing with the three sisters." The sisters—reading, writing and spelling—must all "dance" to the same music. If you are using a developmental approach in your reading and writing instruction, then spelling and vocabulary instruction should not utilize a memorization model. We refer you to our first book, *Teaching and Assessing Spelling* (Scholastic,

2002) for guidance in assessing your students. This resource provides the assessment tool the Spelling Knowledge Inventory (SKI). This formal assessment:

- mirrors the developmental phases.
- targets students' global understandings about words.
- is flexible enough to accommodate the ebb and flow of student spelling development.
- provides multiple opportunities to assess.

In keeping our eye on the child, the assessment provides guidance in selecting which word features would be most beneficial for students to work with. The very reason we teach spelling is to help students become independent writers with dependable tools to use. In planning spelling and word study instruction, what teachers are assessing is evidence of what students already understand, what they are currently grappling with, and what is still beyond their knowledge base. Just as in all areas of literacy instruction, it takes careful observation and assessment to guide instructional planning. Educators know new growth will not occur if the student is already operating at an independent level and in turn, they cannot learn if instruction is at the frustration level.

How the book is organized

This book takes you on a tour of the history of the English language with Eddy and Molly Gee©, our etymology twins. Eddy and Molly explore how the Germanic language and Greek and Latin roots influence our language. The twins will explain in "user-friendly" terms common dictionary abbreviations so you can help students explore word origins. Thirty-five Greek and Latin root trees provide models of how to explore relationships between the meanings and spellings of words. Next, we share hundreds of word histories in Chapter 2 followed in Chapter 3 by fifty fascinating idioms, those curious expressions we use. Finally, Chapter 4 is organized by word features with developmentally appropriate lists.

Word study is a fun and fascinating exploration that enriches students' learning and our teaching. We have found our love of words is infectious. Everyone who knows us is constantly bringing us stories that begin…did you know? Once you begin your discovery of our language, you create new bonds with other learners, old and young. Many times the stories they share with us are a surprise, but most often we find ourselves saying, "Ah-ha, well that makes sense…." We hope you will share your stories with us, too.

Words have a longer life than deeds.
—Pindar (518 BCE–438 BCE), Nemean Odes

Chapter 1
A Short History of the English Language With 35 Word Trees of Greek and Latin Roots

Broadly speaking, the short words are the best,
and the old words best of all.
—Sir Winston Churchill (1874–1965)

It's human nature to enjoy a good story. Every word in the English language traveled over time and distance. Sharing entertaining word stories with students will entice them to begin an exploration of their own. Understanding the history of English does not require a degree in linguistics! We offer a way to share a bit of history with children via the conversation between two spunky siblings. We would like you to meet our adventurous and curious twins, Eddy and Molly Gee© (etymology—the history of words) who globe-trot their way to discover how English came to be. Read it aloud, adapt it, role-play…but most importantly, enjoy the adventure with your students.

Our word sleuthing twins, Eddy and Molly Gee©, with dictionaries, time lines, and maps packed in their suitcases, are ready to search the world for the birthplace of the words we use today. No Fodor's or Frommer's for these two, the trusty dictionary is their travel guide. Using the information provided, they are able to travel back to the beginnings of many words and discover surprising "birth-places" along the way. For example, Eddy and Molly have been told many times that they are two very "curious" children…so they decide to look that one up! Opening her *Webster's Third New International Dictionary* (unabridged), Molly found on page 556 the entry for "curious." She saw:

cu·ri·ous \'kyůrēəs, -ür-\ *adj, sometimes* -ER/-EST [ME, fr. MF *curios,* fr. L *curiosus* careful, inquisitive, fr. *curi-* (fr. *cura* care) + *-osus* -ous — more at CURE] **1 a** *archaic* **:** made or prepared with careful skill **:** elaborately or exquisitely executed **:** DAINTY, ELABORATE, RECHERCHÉ **b** *obs* **:** minutely searching **:** ABSTRUSE, RECONDITE **c** *archaic* **:** marked by precise accuracy or careful ingenuity **d** *now dial* **:** CHOICE, EXCELLENT, SUPERLATIVE **2 a :** marked by desire to investigate and learn **:** showing interest in finding or searching out information **:** INQUISITIVE ⟨a rationalist who was ∼ and had a sort of scientific interest in life —D.H.Lawrence⟩ ⟨a man, like a cat, is ∼ about his environment and keeps investigating it —Stuart Chase⟩ **b :** given to investigating concerns other than one's own ⟨an apprentice ∼ of his master's secrets⟩; *often* **:** marked by inquisitiveness about others' concerns **:** PRYING, NOSY ⟨∼ about the neighbors' doings⟩ **c** *archaic* **:** having a connoisseur's or virtuoso's interests **3 a** *now dial* **:** difficult to please **:** FASTIDIOUS **b** *archaic* **:** CAREFUL, SOLICITOUS, CHARY, CAUTIOUS **4 a** *archaic* **:** accompanied by feelings of interest **:** INTERESTING **b :** exciting attention, inquiry, speculation, or surprise as strange, hard to explain, unusual, or novel **:** awakening inquisitiveness **:** EXTRAORDINARY ⟨whatever we're thoroughly unfamiliar with is apt to seem to us odd . . . or ∼—J.L.Lowes⟩ **c** *of a book*
syn INQUISITIVE, PRYING, SNOOPY, NOSY: CURIOUS always suggests an eager desire to learn and may or may not imply such objectionable qualities as intrusiveness or impertinence ⟨a *curious* person, who searches into things under the earth and in heaven —Benjamin Jowett⟩ ⟨anyone who is prematurely *curious* to see the difference in treatment between different centuries —Henry Adams⟩ ⟨it was as if listening to her I had

"Wow, Molly," said Eddy, "what do you think all that means?"

Molly pointed to the text and explained to Eddy the following:

"See Eddy," said Molly, pointing to the entry. "Each part of this tells us something important about the word. Just like you and I have a passport that records where we started and where we have traveled, the etymology entry in a dictionary is a sort of 'passport' for our words."

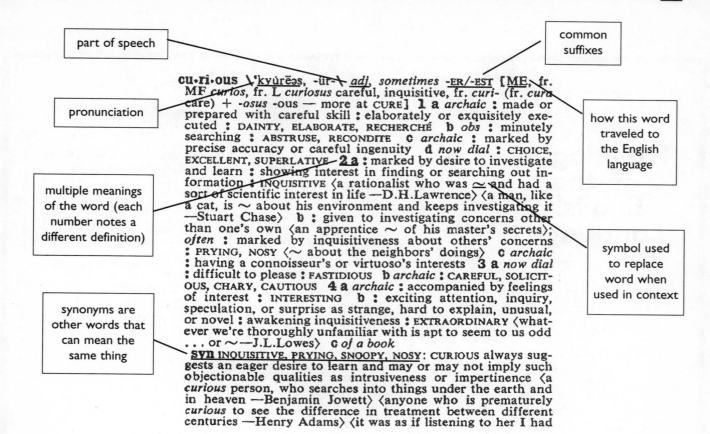

part of speech

pronunciation

common suffixes

how this word traveled to the English language

multiple meanings of the word (each number notes a different definition)

symbol used to replace word when used in context

synonyms are other words that can mean the same thing

cu·ri·ous \'kyúrēəs, -úr-\ *adj, sometimes* -ER/-EST [ME, fr. MF *curios*, fr. L *curiosus* careful, inquisitive, fr. curi- (fr. *cura* care) + -osus -ous — more at CURE] **1 a** *archaic* : made or prepared with careful skill : elaborately or exquisitely executed : DAINTY, ELABORATE, RECHERCHÉ **b** *obs* : minutely searching : ABSTRUSE, RECONDITE **c** *archaic* : marked by precise accuracy or careful ingenuity **d** *now dial* : CHOICE, EXCELLENT, SUPERLATIVE **2 a** : marked by desire to investigate and learn : showing interest in finding or searching out information : INQUISITIVE ⟨a rationalist who was ∼ and had a sort of scientific interest in life —D.H.Lawrence⟩ ⟨a man, like a cat, is ∼ about his environment and keeps investigating it —Stuart Chase⟩ **b** : given to investigating concerns other than one's own ⟨an apprentice ∼ of his master's secrets⟩; *often* : marked by inquisitiveness about others' concerns : PRYING, NOSY ⟨∼ about the neighbors' doings⟩ **c** *archaic* : having a connoisseur's or virtuoso's interests **3 a** *now dial* : difficult to please : FASTIDIOUS **b** *archaic* : CAREFUL, SOLICITOUS, CHARY, CAUTIOUS **4 a** *archaic* : accompanied by feelings of interest : INTERESTING **b** : exciting attention, inquiry, speculation, or surprise as strange, hard to explain, unusual, or novel : awakening inquisitiveness : EXTRAORDINARY ⟨whatever we're thoroughly unfamiliar with is apt to seem to us odd . . . or ∼ —J.L.Lowes⟩ **c** *of a book*
syn INQUISITIVE, PRYING, SNOOPY, NOSY: CURIOUS always suggests an eager desire to learn and may or may not imply such objectionable qualities as intrusiveness or impertinence ⟨a *curious* person, who searches into things under the earth and in heaven —Benjamin Jowett⟩ ⟨anyone who is prematurely *curious* to see the difference in treatment between different centuries —Henry Adams⟩ ⟨it was as if listening to her I had

"I see Molly," said Eddy, "that the countries have abbreviations…the front of the dictionary tells what each of those mean. Let's make a list of those so we can find them on the map each time we find a new and interesting word."

L = Latin
Gk = Greek
F = French (OF = Old French)
G = German
ME = Middle English
OE = Old English
Du = Dutch
Celt = Celtic
IE = Indo-European
It = Italian
Sp = Spanish
Sw = Swedish

"Gee, Molly, I understand that the abbreviations are for the language and the country the word came from…and I can figure out most of the them. Like, Old English would be from England and Greek would be from Greece. But, where's Latin on the map?"

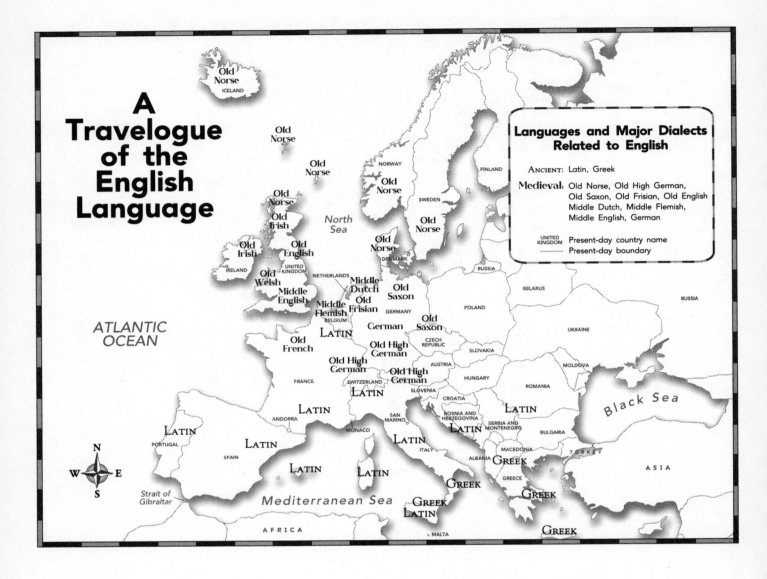

A Travelogue of the English Language

Languages and Major Dialects Related to English

ANCIENT: Latin, Greek

MEDIEVAL: Old Norse, Old High German, Old Saxon, Old Frisian, Old English Middle Dutch, Middle Flemish, Middle English, German

UNITED KINGDOM — Present-day country name
- - - - - Present-day boundary

"I know where we can find out…the dictionary!" exclaims Molly.

Molly and Eddy find that *Latin* is described as being derived from *Latinus*, the ancient country of Italy, which had Rome as its capital. Languages that stemmed from Latin are known as Romance languages. Eddy and Molly found Rome, Italy on the map and soon discover that many words have both Latin and Greek origins. The twins decide to do a little time travel to see how English got to where it is today. They find a travelogue of the English language (or a language map like the one shown above) and a time line of the development of the English language (like the following historical chronology) and away they go!

The Spelling List and Word Study Resource Book · Scholastic Professional Books

Chronology of the history of English

Date	Historical events	Language
55 & 54 BCE	Julius Caesar lands	Celtic
43	Roman conquest begins	Celtic & Latin
End of 3rd c.	Attacks by Germanic tribes	Romanized Celtic & Germanic
383–410	Withdrawal of Roman troops	
449	Germanic invasions	Scattered Germanic settlements
c. 547	Anglian kingdom north of Humber	
597	Augustine starts christianization in Kent	Largely Germanic
634	Irish monks christianize Northumbria	
655	Christianization of Mercia completed	
664	Synod of Whitby	
c. 725	Beowulf	Anglo-Saxon
787	First wave of Danish invasions	
865	Second wave of Danish invasions	
886	Sovereignty of Alfred the Great	
964	Monastic reform	Standardization of Old English
973	Edgar crowned king of England	
991	Third wave of Danish invasions	
1066	Norman conquest	Norman French official language
1204	Normandy lost	
1258	Royal proclamation in English	English official language
1348–1350	The Black Death	
1362	Parliament opened in English	
1382	Peasants' Revolt	
1476	Caxton's printing press in Westminster	
1531	Henry VIIIth breaks with Rome Bible translations	
1588	Bullokar's Pamphlet for Grammar	Standardization
1607	English brought to America (Virginia)	American English
1639–1686	English settlements in India	English as a trading language
1664	Royal Society: committee	Standardization
1759	Quebec gained	
1761	India a colony	
1805	Battle of Trafalgar	
1816	First inexpensive newspaper	Mass media
1858	Beginning of work on NED (later OED)	
19th c.	Technical progress	Scientific language
1899–1901	Boer War	English in South Africa
1914–1918	World War I	English as language of diplomacy
1939–1945	World War II	Spread of American English

source: http://coral.lili.unibielefeld.de/Classes/Winter96/Dialects/dialects/node32.html

A brief historical time line

The twins begin their journey five- to seven-thousand years ago.

Groups who lived in inland Eastern Europe were called Indo-Europeans. By 3500 B.C.E. the Indo-Europeans migrated to Northwest Europe. By 2000 B.C.E. they had moved into Greece and then on to Italy.

"Of course, Eddy," said Molly, "wherever they went, they took their spoken language with them! By 200 B.C.E. they moved into what is now Poland and Germany. Their language shifted as they took on the Germanic sounds of the language spoken by the people who lived in the area they migrated to."

"Hey, Molly, I read that the 100 most frequently used words in our speech are all Germanic. And of the next 100 we use, 83 are also Germanic."

"Wow, that's amazing. The Germanic words are so old and they've really influenced our language."

Looking at both the time line and map, the curious twins discover that at 43 B.C.E. the Romans began a conquering spree. One area they invaded was Greece. Further reading shows the twins that the upper-class Romans learned Greek, which eventually led to the absorption of many Greek words into the Latin language. In 55 B.C.E., the Romans invaded what is now the British Isles. The people were the Celts, but they had little influence on the Latin-speaking Romans. Latin was used for educational and religious purposes in this region, but was not used by the common peasant. The colony of "Britannia" was established by 43 C.E.

"Hey, Molly, I saw in the dictionary a bunch of words called 'Old English.' When was that?" Molly suggested that they time travel to 410 C.E.

Arriving in 410 C.E. they see that the Roman Empire had started to crumble, so the Romans moved out of Britannia to help defend other regions. The first Germanic tribes soon arrived in Britannia—these were the Angles, Saxons, Jute, and some Frisians. Their Germanic language was distantly related to Latin due to their earlier contact with the Romans.

"Eddy, I see in the dictionary that 449 C.E. is called the 'Old English' period…and the time line shows that's when the Angles and Saxons moved into Britain."

"Yes, Molly, and I looked up the word *English* and it's from *Engla land* meaning the land of the Angles which became England…so that's why what we speak is called English!"

When the twins arrive in 793 C.E., the Vikings (Norsemen) have invaded Britain. They settled there and married the peasants, bringing along their language, which had similar Germanic roots. This developed into the Old English period of our language.

"So Molly, I see on the map 'Old Norse.' Why is that important?" Eddy wants to know.

"Well, Eddy, the Vikings created some subtle changes in the inflection of words already being used in Britain and they also added some new words, like *window* and *sister*."

"Molly, the dictionary says *window* is from the Old Norse and means wind eye. I bet that had something to do with how they built their homes. I see that *sister* meant the same thing in the Old Norse as it does in English."

The twins travel ahead to the time of what is now called Middle English. This period followed the

1066 C.E. Norman conquests. William the Conqueror (the Duke of Normandy) took over the throne of England. French became the language of the ruling class. Latin still played an important part in education and the church (as it did in France), but the common people still spoke a Germanic-based English. The majority spoke English, but they absorbed about 10,000 French words (75 percent of which we still use today) into their language. The Plague, which killed more than a third of the population from 1347 to 1351, created a change in the ruling class. Survivors mainly spoke the language of the peasants. That's when Old English and French blended, beginning the Middle English period.

"I wondered about the word *perspiring* the other day when the teacher used it in gym class," said Eddy. "I looked it up and it has French roots. So I looked up sweat, which means the same thing...it has Germanic roots."

"Right, Eddy. Remember, the ruling class spoke French and the peasants spoke their Germanic-based language. That's why we have two Modern English words that mean the same thing, like venison or deer and poultry or chicken."

The twins look back at their time line, noticing that in 1476, William Caxton brought the printing press to London. The printing press allowed conventions of language to take root. Before that, there were no standardized spellings, because scribes handwrote much of the "print" and the Norman scribes changed some words to fit their pronunciation. By the1500s, books became less expensive and more plentiful. More and more people learned to read.

"So, Molly, once the printing press created these conventions, the way a word was spelled stopped changing, but how it might have been pronounced did not."

"Right, Eddy. For instance, some medieval words had the "silent *e*" pronounced at the end...but we do not say them that way now."

The Renaissance, from 1500 to 1800 C.E., brought a whole new interest in the Greek and Latin languages and many words were added to English. Since the demand for books was so high, Latin texts were translated into English. Many Latin words were used where no English word could be found.

"Molly, the dictionary has information about 'The Great Vowel Shift' during this time. What's that?"

"Since we have traveled to 1500 C.E., the dictionary says we have moved into the 'Early Modern English Period.' The Great Vowel Shift primarily changed the sounds of the long vowels. For example, before, in Middle English, the word *go* rhymed with the word *law*, but in Modern English it rhymes with *low*. Believe it or not, *good* rhymed with *rode* instead of *hood*. It's a mystery even today why just a few generations of English speakers created this shift. Nobody knows why it happened."

Early Modern English continued to develop as its use spread and more borrowing occurred. The language went wherever the speakers went...it was one of the most treasured items they carried in their travels to England's new colonies. These English travelers also learned new words wherever they went.

"Molly, I remember when we studied about the colonies and how the American Indians helped the new settlers. The colonists learned new words from the American Indian words like *moose* and *skunk*."

"Right you are, Eddy, and the English language continues to grow and change. Just think of all the new technology words we have that our parents had never heard of when they were our age."

So Eddy and Molly Gee return home, excited to explore the historic travels taken by words they know…and the map is right in the dictionary!

Family trees of language

As Molly and Eddy discovered through their historical journey, the Ancient Greeks and Romans not only influenced each other's language, but that of many other countries as well. Those languages were brought to England and the richness of our language began. So now Eddy and Molly can begin to check the "passport" of some everyday words. Where did these words start? What did their root mean and what other words are related?

The following section has "family trees" of words you might use in your classroom during the year. The power of these trees is that they help students see all of a word's ancestors—the relationships among words—both in terms of their spellings and their meanings. We encourage you to add to the trees any related words you find as you teach. Glossaries and vocabulary lists you already have are wonderful resources for further word discoveries that have particular interests for your students. Word webs such as these can be left posted in your classroom all year for students to add to as they find related words.

To us, this kind of exploration marks the intersection of spelling and word study instruction. For example, the digraph /ch/ is sometimes pronounced /k/. This comes directly to our language from the Greeks. Words such as *chemistry, chaos, archive, chrome, chronic,* and *Christmas* stem from Greek roots. At the same time, /ch/ can also be pronounced /sh/. This French influence is heard is such words as *chalet, chagrin, Charlotte, Champagne, Chicago,* and *chauffeur.* And yet again, the /ch/ can be pronounced /ch/ as in *chain, church, children, chair, lunch* and *coach* from the Old English. When a /gh/ is silent (such as in *fight, high, bought, naughty*), it can be traced directly to the Anglo-Saxon. Words that begin /sk/ or /sc/ find their heritage with the Old Norse (such as *skin, sky, scatter, scold*). When there is a silent /p/ at the beginning of the word, it is Greek (such as *pneumonia* and *psychology*), just as is the /f/ sound of /ph/ in words such as *philosophy* and *phone.*

Understanding the origin of a word can demystify words once called "demons" and can replace our impression that the English language is unpredictable with the realization that spelling patterns have a logical and, perhaps, long history.

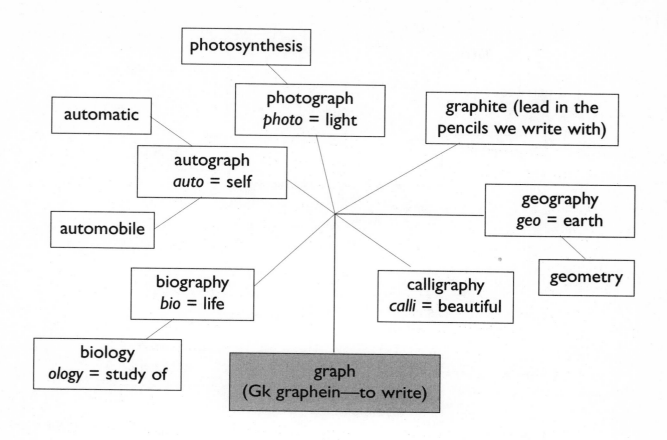

photosynthesis

photograph
photo = light

graphite (lead in the pencils we write with)

automatic

autograph
auto = self

automobile

geography
geo = earth

geometry

biography
bio = life

calligraphy
calli = beautiful

biology
ology = study of

graph
(Gk graphein—to write)

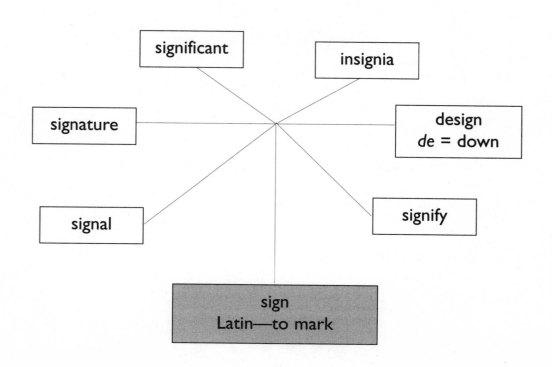

significant

insignia

signature

design
de = down

signal

signify

sign
Latin—to mark

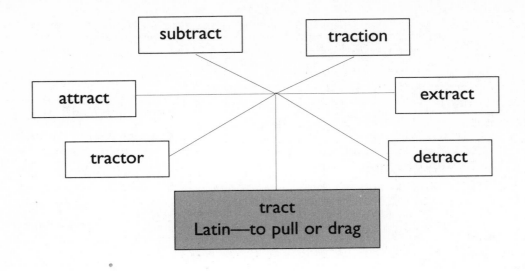

subtract

traction

attract

extract

tractor

detract

tract
Latin—to pull or drag

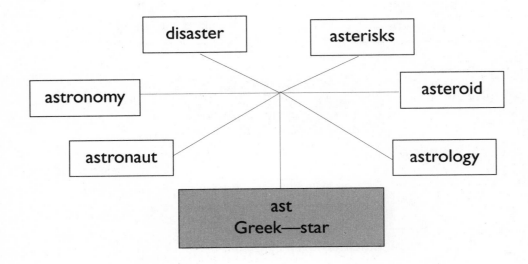

disaster

asterisks

astronomy

asteroid

astronaut

astrology

ast
Greek—star

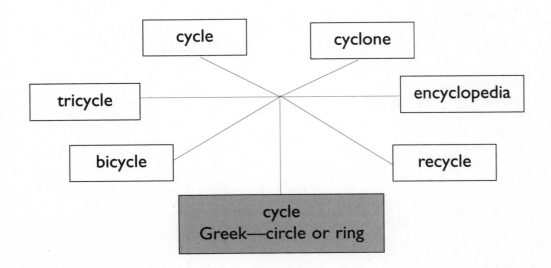

cycle

cyclone

tricycle

encyclopedia

bicycle

recycle

cycle
Greek—circle or ring

The Spelling List and Word Study Resource Book · Scholastic Professional Books

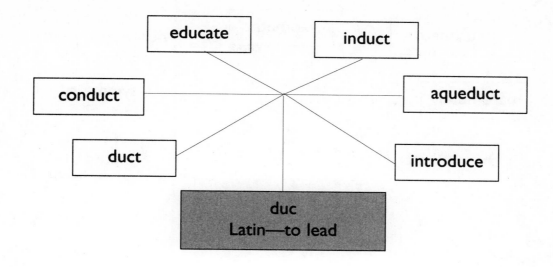

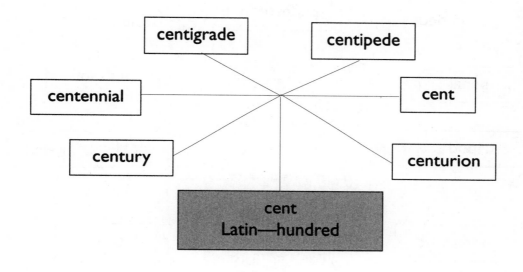

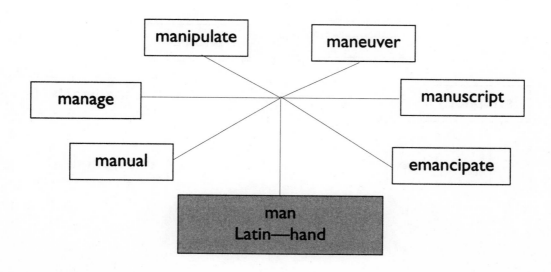

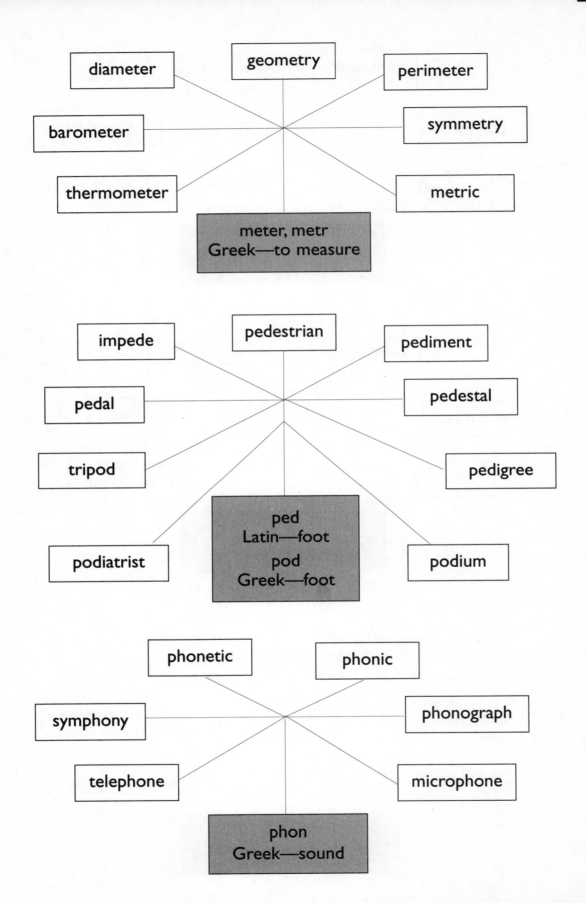

diameter

geometry

perimeter

barometer

symmetry

thermometer

metric

**meter, metr
Greek—to measure**

impede

pedestrian

pediment

pedal

pedestal

tripod

pedigree

podiatrist

**ped
Latin—foot
pod
Greek—foot**

podium

phonetic

phonic

symphony

phonograph

telephone

microphone

**phon
Greek—sound**

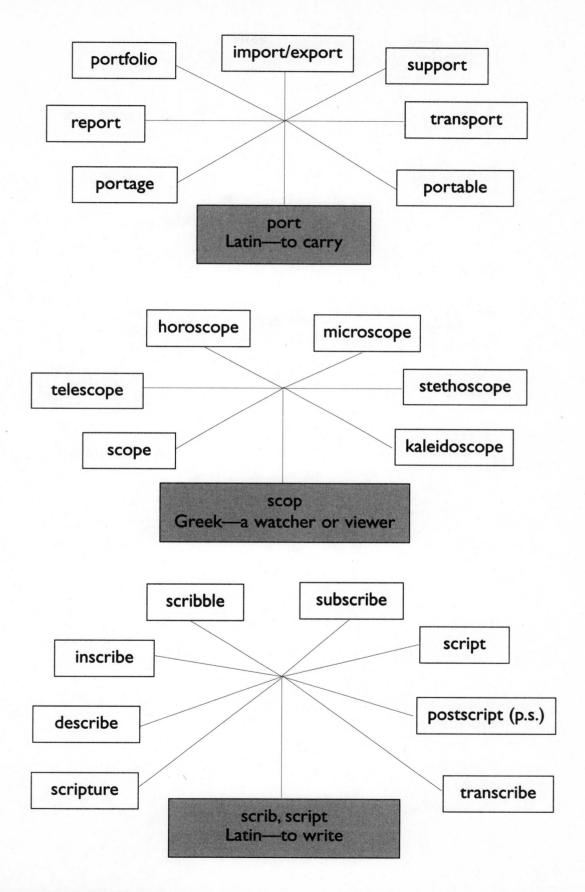

portfolio

import/export

support

report

transport

portage

portable

port
Latin—to carry

horoscope

microscope

telescope

stethoscope

scope

kaleidoscope

scop
Greek—a watcher or viewer

scribble

subscribe

inscribe

script

describe

postscript (p.s.)

scripture

transcribe

scrib, script
Latin—to write

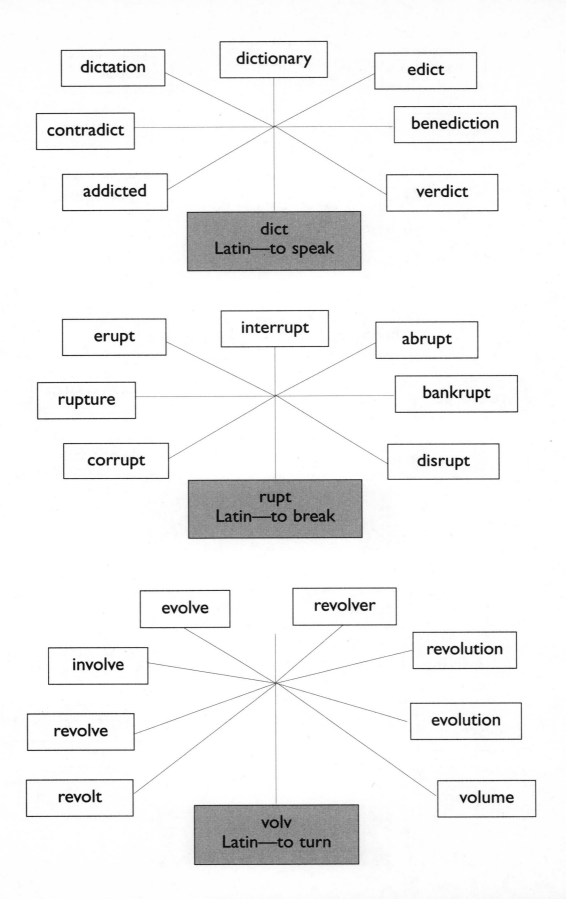

dictation

dictionary

edict

contradict

benediction

addicted

verdict

dict
Latin—to speak

erupt

interrupt

abrupt

rupture

bankrupt

corrupt

disrupt

rupt
Latin—to break

evolve

revolver

involve

revolution

revolve

evolution

revolt

volume

volv
Latin—to turn

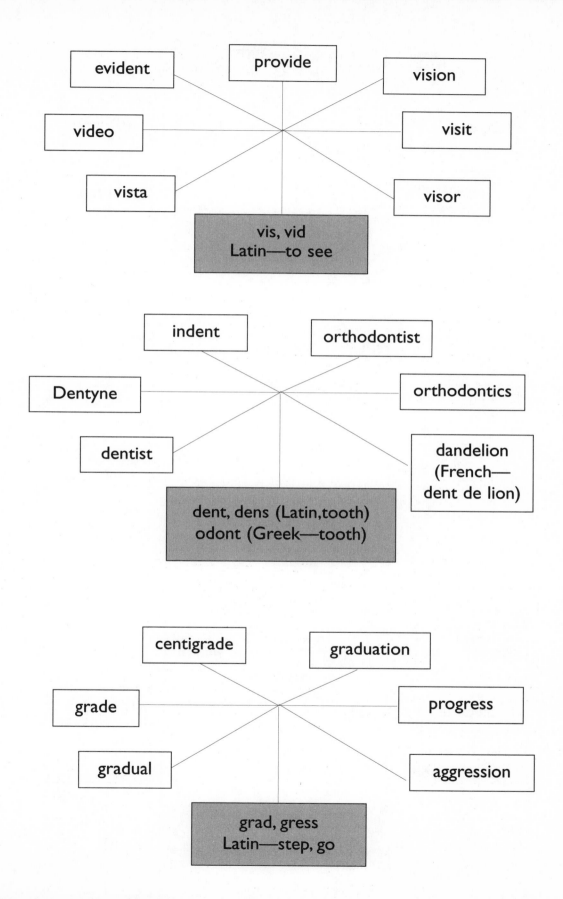

evident

provide

vision

video

visit

vista

visor

**vis, vid
Latin—to see**

indent

orthodontist

Dentyne

orthodontics

dentist

dandelion
(French—
dent de lion)

**dent, dens (Latin, tooth)
odont (Greek—tooth)**

centigrade

graduation

grade

progress

gradual

aggression

**grad, gress
Latin—step, go**

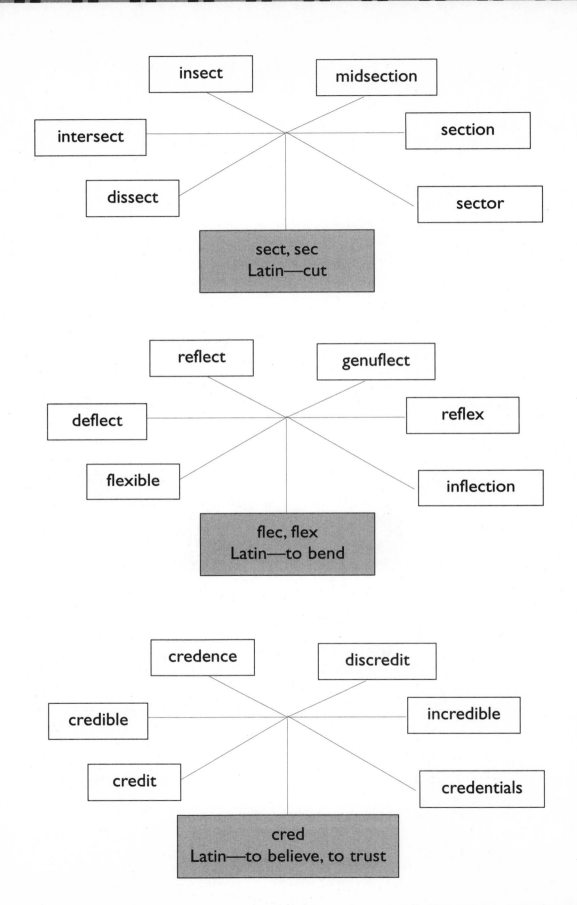

insect

midsection

intersect

section

dissect

sector

**sect, sec
Latin—cut**

reflect

genuflect

deflect

reflex

flexible

inflection

**flec, flex
Latin—to bend**

credence

discredit

credible

incredible

credit

credentials

**cred
Latin—to believe, to trust**

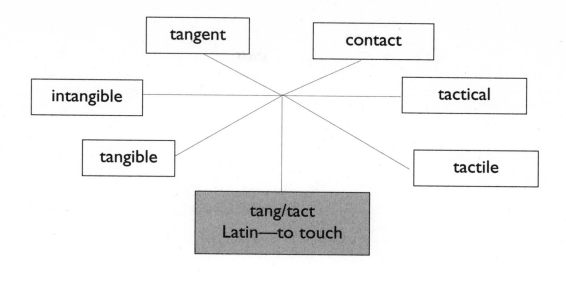

tangent

contact

intangible

tactical

tangible

tactile

tang/tact
Latin—to touch

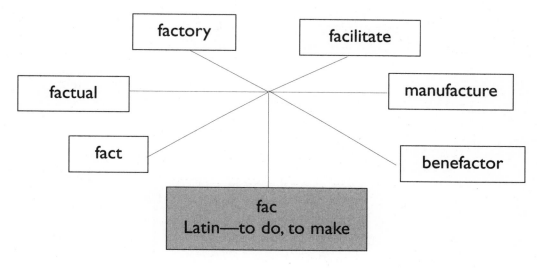

factory

facilitate

factual

manufacture

fact

benefactor

fac
Latin—to do, to make

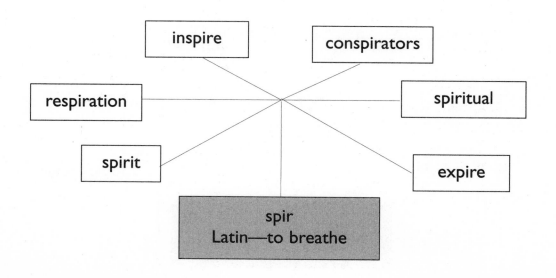

inspire

conspirators

respiration

spiritual

spirit

expire

spir
Latin—to breathe

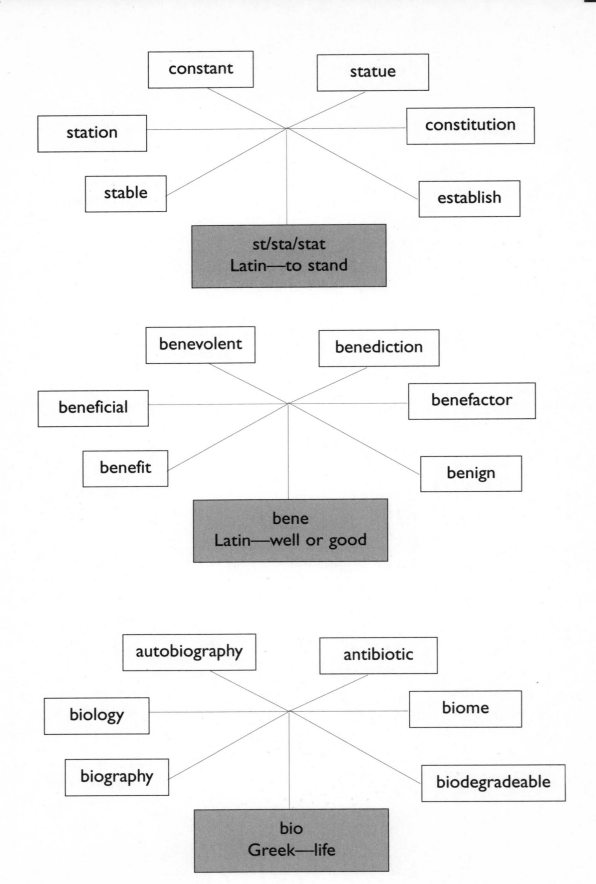

constant

statue

station

constitution

stable

establish

st/sta/stat
Latin—to stand

benevolent

benediction

beneficial

benefactor

benefit

benign

bene
Latin—well or good

autobiography

antibiotic

biology

biome

biography

biodegradeable

bio
Greek—life

The Spelling List and Word Study Resource Book · Scholastic Professional Books

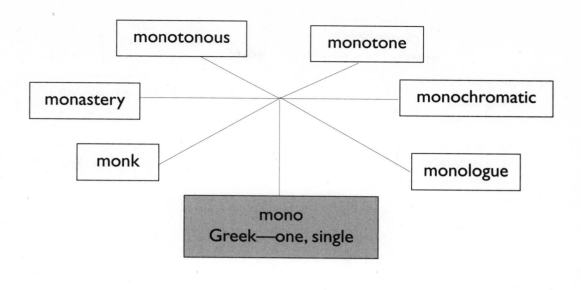

monotonous

monotone

monastery

monochromatic

monk

monologue

mono
Greek—one, single

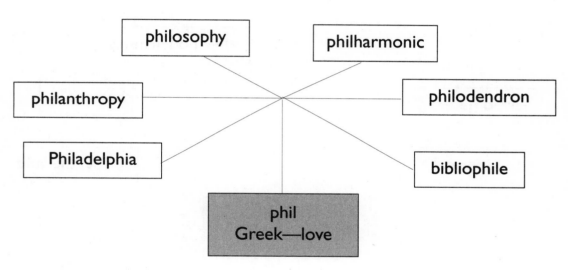

philosophy

philharmonic

philanthropy

philodendron

Philadelphia

bibliophile

phil
Greek—love

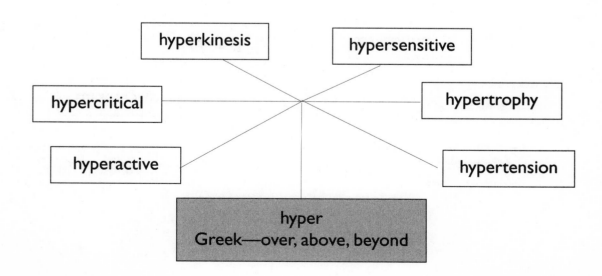

hyperkinesis

hypersensitive

hypercritical

hypertrophy

hyperactive

hypertension

hyper
Greek—over, above, beyond

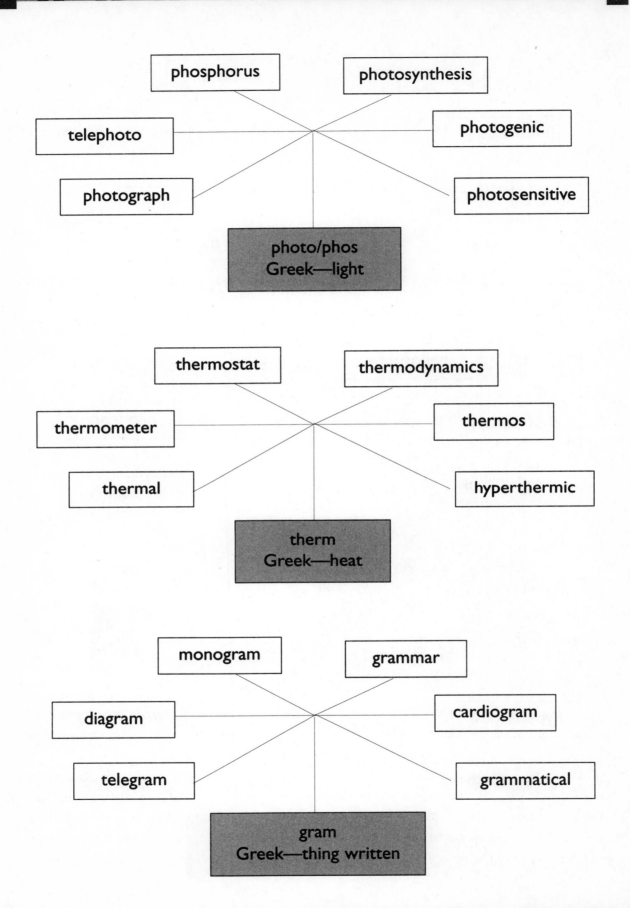

phosphorus

photosynthesis

telephoto

photogenic

photograph

photosensitive

**photo/phos
Greek—light**

thermostat

thermodynamics

thermometer

thermos

thermal

hyperthermic

**therm
Greek—heat**

monogram

grammar

diagram

cardiogram

telegram

grammatical

**gram
Greek—thing written**

Chapter 2
Word Histories for the Classroom:
320 Hand-picked Stories, Eponyms, and Acronyms

Words are the leaves of the tree of language, of which, if some fall away,
a new succession takes their place.
—Field Marshal John French (1852–1925)

As we've begun to discover, words in the English language come with a past that reads much like a historical novel, complete with conquests, colorful conquerors, rich folk and, last but not least, common folk, all of whom keep the language alive and changing.

Some words reflect past beliefs about nature and deities. The days of the week are a good example of this. The Romans first named them after the planets because they believed a planet ruled the first hour of each day. However, when the Saxons invaded, they renamed some days for their Germanic gods. Middle English speakers then translated the Roman and Saxon names they heard. For example, the Saxons' "Sun's Day," or sacred day of the sun, was combined into *Sunday*. The Saxon's supreme god was Woden and the fourth day named "Woden's Day." Thus the Middle English speakers heard this as *Wednesday*. When the Quakers organized in the 1600s they chose to call the days of the week First Day, Second Day, and so on rather than use the words they knew had pagan origins. The Quakers continue today to use these names for the week days.

The English language is an interesting tapestry woven by many cultures. So how was this interesting tapestry woven? What are the strands that provide the richness of our language? There are six:

1. The first strand reflects **historical conquests.** During military movements, conquering peoples brought their language and culture with them. Conquered people adopted certain words that helped them to survive. As these words were added, changes were made to align with the conquered peoples' own pronunciations and spellings. The evolution of the days of the week is an example.

2. Second, some words are **mistakes.** This was due to the mishearing of the subtleties of a spoken language. For example, *Connecticut* was the Mohican name for river, *quinnitukqut*. When English speakers heard this word, they pronounced it with sounds they were familiar with and able to reproduce. They believed they were pronouncing it as they heard it. This pronunciation continued and once the word needed to be written, English spelling patterns were assigned to what they heard. So, over time, the written form no longer resembled the Mohican word.

3. Other words were **misinterpretations.** As words traveled over time, changing in pronunciation and spelling, further changes occurred as a word made its final appearance in English. How the word traveled and who brought it to English had impact on its current use. Our word, *dollar,* originated in the 16th century with minted coins in a Bohemian town called *Joachymov.* The coins were called *joachmistaler* which the Germans shortened to *taler.* The Dutch called it *daler.* The United States misinterpreted *daler* to mean any currency, thus naming our monetary unit *dollar.*

4. Words came from **people's names.** One of the great perks of inventing something is the opportunity to name it after yourself. Many words we use are, in fact, names of people involved in a product or doing a deed. These words are called eponyms Next time you eat a graham cracker, thank Sylvester Graham, a 19th-century Presbyterian minister who was active in the temperance movement. He traveled the United States promoting a healthful diet and pure living. While graham crackers are said to be made of graham flour, simple whole-wheat flour is actually used. Even today, a graham cracker is considered a healthful snack…named for Rev. Graham, the promoter of dietary reform.

5. Next, words are invented by **combining words.** Lewis Caroll, author of *Alice in Wonderland,* created new words and named them *portmanteaus.* For example, if you say you are *flabbergasted* (*flap + aghast*) by the events *telecasted* (*television + broadcast*) on a *sitcom* (*situation + comedy*), you have just used three portmanteaus. Acronyms are formed by the first letters or groups of letters of words

in a phrase and are combined to become a pronounceable word. An example of this is PIN (personal identification number).

6. And finally, words **evolved from other words.** Spellings and meanings of some words have evolved over time. A good example of this is the word *good-bye*. This changed in both meaning and spelling. Originally, in the 16th century, the saying was *God be with ye*. By the 18th century it had evolved to *good-bye*.

What sparks a word study? Interest in a word or phrase can send us on a journey to solve the mystery of what and where. Why do we use the phrase *chewing the fat* to describe sitting around talking with our friends? Why are your jeans made of denim? How long have people been hemming and hawing? What does elbow have to do with math? And what's so funny about a funny bone anyway?

This book is not about your old vocabulary memorization lesson: it's all about stories. People tend to repeat stories that are entertaining or memorable to them in some way. We hope you will repeat these stories (and more) to your students. Expect the unexpected! Now, let's tell some stories about the fabric of our language.

Hundreds of Word Histories, Acronyms, and Portmanteaus

The words selected for this section are ones that appear in grades 1 through 6 curriculums in schools we have worked with. Many are words that students themselves have brought to our attention.

WORD HISTORIES

agriculture—from the Latin words *agri* (field) and *cultura* (cultivation), meaning "tilling the field."

Alabama—named for original inhabitants, the *Alpaamo*.

Alaska—a Russian pronunciation of the Inuit word *alaxsxaqu*, which means "mainland."

algebra—from the Arabic *al-jebr* (reuniting) or *jabara* (to reunite). First used to mean bone setting. During the Middle Ages, the word changed from the longer Arabic phrase *ilm al-jebr wa'lmuqobalah* to become the mathematical term *algebra,* meaning "reuniting" or "equating."

alibi—from the Latin *alius,* meaning other (as does *alias*).

alphabet—from the names of the first two letters of the Greek alphabet, *alpha* and *beta.* The Greeks used these two letters to talk about their alphabet, much like we refer to our ABCs.

America—after Amerigo Vespucci, in the belief that he was the first explorer to reach the mainland of what is now the United States.

amuse—from the Old French *amuser* (to waste time). This changed when used in English to mean "to delude" or "entertain." Related word: *amusement* (the act of being amused).

animal—from the Latin *animal,* meaning "breath." If we animate something, we make it alive.

antler—from the Latin *ramum ant ocularis,* meaning "the branch before the eyes." The French referred to it as *antoillier* and the English heard it as *antler.*

April—based on the Latin word *aperio,* meaning "open." The Roman name was *Aprilis,* the month of the first flowers opening in ancient Italy.

arena—derived from the Latin *harena,* meaning "sand." In ancient times, arenas had floors of sand and were located near butcher stores because they were where animals were slaughtered. The sand absorbed the animals' blood. Now *arena* refers to an area designated for entertainment or competition.

Arizona—from the Papago *arishoonak,* meaning "small spring place;" changed by the Spanish to *Arizonac.* The Papago were a tribe that lived on the desert in and around what is now Arizona.

Arkansas—from the Sioux *Arkansa,* meaning "south wind people." The French added the final silent *s.*

astronomy—from the Greek *astronomia*—from *astro,* meaning "star" and *nomia,* meaning "to observe."

athlete—from the Latin *athleta* and the Greek *athletes,* meaning "to contend for a prize."

August—was originally *Sextilis*, the sixth month of the Roman calendar. In 8 B.C.E. the Roman senate renamed the month *Augustus* to honor Augustus Caesar, the first emperor of Rome. The English changed the spelling to *August*.

aware—from the Old English *i war* and from the Middle English *awar* meaning "to be on one's guard."

badminton—named for Badminton House in Gloucestershire, the estate of the Duke of Beaufort, where the game was played in the late 1800s. The Duke brought the game to England from India. The sport dates back at least 2,000 years to the games of battledore and shuttlecock, which were played in ancient Greece, India, and China.

basketball—invented by Dr. James Naismith. A Canadian, Naismith was teaching physical education at the International Young Men's Christian Training College in Springfield, Massachusetts, in 1891. He needed an activity to keep the young men busy during the winter months. He cut the bottoms out of peach baskets, hung them, and challenged students to move a ball down the gym floor and throw it through the basket.

black—from the Old English *blaec* or *blac,* meaning "dusky" or "ink."

blimp—from England. Floating balloons were classified as rigid and non-rigid. In the early 1900s, the English were attempting to invent a better non-rigid balloon to use for military and civilian purposes, such as travel, weather, and surveillance. The test models were labeled using letters of the alphabet. The first limp (or non-rigid) balloon, called "Plan A," was unsuccessful. The second attempt, better known as the "B-limp," was successful and lent its test name to the final product—the *blimp*.

blue—from the Middle English *bleu,* for the color.

Braille—printing for the blind, named for the inventor, Louis Braille.

boycott—to refuse the use of something as a form of objection or protest. Named for Captain C.C. Boycott, an Irish land agent who raised the rent on his tenants in 1880. To protest, they refused to sell him anything and blocked his mail and food supplies.

caboose—derived from the Dutch *kombias,* meaning "ship's galley." Dutch seamen of Medieval times were daring and often went on long sailing adventures. They needed a kitchen (or galley) on board. In 1860, the word was used for the last car on the train because this word came to mean cookroom.

California—named by first Spanish settlers in the 1500s. *Calafia*, an imaginary treasure island, was the setting of a popular Spanish folktale.

candidate—from the Latin *candidatus,* meaning "person dressed in white." Early Roman politicians wore white togas to make a good impression; we now associate the word with a person seeking political office. Related words: *incandescent* (to become white) and *candid* (straightforward).

candy—from the Sanskrit *kahanda,* meaning a "piece" of something; then to the Italian *candi,* meaning "lump of sugar;" and finally to the current English spelling and meaning.

canoe—from the word of Caribbean origin *kanoa,* meaning "dug out" or "hollow log." Columbus brought the word back to Spain, where the spelling changed.

civic—from the Latin *civicus* or *civis,* meaning "citizen." Related words: *city, civilian, civil.*

coconut—from the Spanish and Portuguese *coco,* meaning "grimace." Sailors who first saw cococuts thought they looked like grimacing faces.

college—from the Latin *col,* meaning "together" or "with," and *lege* meaning "gather" or "choose."

Colorado—Spanish, meaning "red."

complex—from the Latin *complecti,* meaning "to entwine around."

Connecticut—from the Mohican name for the *Quinnitukqut* river, which means "long tidal river."

corruption—from the Latin *corruptus* and Old French *corrupt. Cor* means "with" or "together" and *rupt* means "break" or "burst."

December—this was originally the tenth month of the Roman calendar, and was thus named *decem,* meaning "ten." This became *decembre* in Old French and Middle English. Latin influenced the spelling of its current form.

deciduous—from the Latin *deciduus: de* means "down" or "away," and *cidere* means "to fall."

Delaware—the name of the first colonial administrator of this region, Baron de la Warr.

denim—derived from Nimes, the city in France where the material (once called *serge de nimes*) was made.

dentist—from the Latin *dent,* meaning "tooth" and *ist,* meaning "one who."

describe—from the Latin *de,* meaning "down" and *script,* meaning "to write." Related words: *scribble, scribe, manuscript,* and *postscript* (*p.s.*).

dictionary—from the Latin *dict,* meaning "to speak" or "to say" and *arium,* meaning "collection." A dictionary is a collection of the words we speak. Related words: *dictaphone, dictate, dictation, predict, edict,* and *verdict.*

dignity—from the Latin *dignitat,* meaning "worthy."

disaster—meaning "against the stars;" from Greek *dis,* meaning "bad" or "ill" and *ast,* meaning "star." Related word: *astrology.*

District of Columbia—named for Christopher Columbus.

doctor—from the Middle Latin *doctor,* meaning "teacher."

dollar—from the name of the small town *Jachymov* in the mountains of northwestern Bohemia where a silver mine was opened in the 16th century. Coins were minted and called *joachimstaler.* In German this became *taler.* Later, the Dutch or Low German form *daler* was borrowed by the English to refer to *taler.* From this, *dollar* was adopted as the name of the U.S. currency.

dumbbell—bell ringing was quite an art during the Middle Ages. But, just as when any other instrument is being learned, novices practiced for hours and not all of it sounded good! So a craftsman invented dumb, or silent, bells which had weighted ropes for clappers and so did not make noise. The weights of the ropes varied, just as the weights of bells did. The dumbbell of today is a silent weight used for physical training just as the novice bell ringers did.

earmark—from Old English. Herdsmen needed a way to mark their cattle (branding was not yet used). When using common pastureland for grazing, they notched the ears of their cattle to signify which belonged to them.

earshot—at one time, land was measured by how far a bow could be shot, and this distance was considered to be "within bowshot." Similarly, anything that was within the range of the human ear began to be called "within earshot."

easel—from the Dutch *ezel*, meaning "donkey." With only three legs, the easel is the poor cousin of the sawhorse, a four-legged stand.

ecology—from the Greek *okologie* meaning "house" or "habitat." Ecology is the study of plants or animals within a habitat.

education—from the Latin *e*, meaning "out" or "from" and *duc*, meaning "to lead."

elbow—from the Latin *ulna* to the Middle English *ell*, specifying a length of fabric. English tailors used the distance between the crook of the arm and the fingertip to measure fabric.

elect—from the Latin *e*, meaning "out" or "from" and *lect*, meaning "to choose."

encyclopedia—from the Greek *egkuklopaideia*, meaning "general education."

envelope—invented in 1714. From the French verb *envelopper*, meaning "covering," "encasing," or "wrapping."

Fahrenheit—named for Gabriel Daniel Fahrenheit, of German descent, born in Poland. He invented the alcohol and mercury thermometers. Fahrenheit experimented with the freezing and boiling points of water and created his scale based on these relative numbers.

family—from the Latin *familia*, meaning "household." Related words: *familiar* and *familiarize*.

February—derived from the Latin *februa*, meaning "spiritual cleansing," which took place at this time of year (added as the second month by the second king of Rome around 700 B.C.E.).

ferris wheel—invented in 1893 by an American engineer named George W. Gale Ferris. The first one was as tall as a 20-story building and each car held 40 riders.

Florida—from Spanish, meaning "land of flowers."

flu—(shortened form of *influenza*) from the Middle Latin *influentia*, meaning "flow from the heavens." Epidemics were once thought to be influenced by the stars. Related words: *influence, influx,* and *influential*.

Frisbee—began as a metal pie tin used at the Frisbie bakery in Bridgeport, Connecticut. Yale University students would eat the pie, then throw the tins to each other for fun. They would yell "Frisbie" to warn others one was coming their way. In the 1950s Wham-O began producing plastic ones and named them Frisbee.

fudge—in the 1890s, a candy maker in Philadelphia was making a batch of caramels. Instead of a chewy confection, his mixture turned into a concoction that melted in his mouth. The candy maker exclaimed "Fudge!" (a common expression of exasperation at the time).

funny bone—this spot that gets a tingly feeling when bumped is at the enlarged end of the humerus bone.

Georgia—named for King George II.

geography—from the Latin and Greek *geographia,* meaning "writing about the earth;" *geo* in Greek means "earth" and *graph* means "to write." Related words: *geometry* (see *meter*) and *geode.*

globe—from the Old French *globe* or the Latin *globus,* meaning "to roll together" or "to stick." Early maps existed only in a flat form, and thus were rolled together.

glossary—from the Greek *glossa,* meaning "tongue" and the Latin *glossa,* meaning "difficult word requiring explanation;" the Latin *arium* means "a collection."

googol—invented by nine-year-old Milton Sirotta when his uncle asked for a word to describe a mathematical number. In the 1930s, Professor Edward Kasner, a mathematician, found himself working with a number so large he had to describe it as 10 to the 100th power. He asked his nephew, Milton, to name this large number, promising he would use Milton's choice when discussing his work. And he did! When he started working with the even larger number of 1 followed by a googol of zeroes, Milton named it *googolplex.*

governor—originally the Greek *kybernao,* meaning "to direct a ship." At that time, the word also took on the meaning of directing the ship of state. The Romans borrowed this word, changing it to *guberno* and taking it with them to France. The meaning remained the same, even after it arrived in the English language as governor.

grade—derived from the Latin *gradatio,* meaning "step."

graffiti—from the Italian *graffito,* meaning "a scratch." Even the walls of Pompeii had *graffiti* (plural of *graffito*). Some that have been translated include "Successus was here," "The fruit sellers ask you to elect Marcus Holconius Priscus as aedile," and "Gaius Julius Primigenius was here. Why are you late?"

gratitude—from the Latin *gratitudo,* meaning "to do a favor" or "make a present of."

green—from the Middle English *grene,* for the color.

gum—from Old French, from Egyptian that came from both Latin and Greek, meaning "palate."

gypsy—from Eastern European countries. These nomadic people were thought to be from Egypt. Thus, first called *egipcien,* later shortened to *gypsy.*

hamburger—derived from the German town, Hamburg, where this steak sandwich was invented.

Hawaii—from the Polynesian *hauaikii*, meaning "home place."

history—from the Greek *hisoria*, or the Latin *historia*, meaning "learning" or "knowing by inquiry."

hogan—from the Navajo (or Dine), meaning "home" or "the home place."

hurricane—from the Taino *huraca'n*, meaning "center of the wind." Christopher Columbus brought this word back to Spain and it eventually made its way into English.

Idaho—from the Shoshone, meaning "good morning" or "gem" or "the mountains."

Illinois—from the Algonquin *ilinwek*, meaning "warriors."

Indiana—the ending *-ana* was added to the original meaning of Indian territory.

infant—from the Latin *in*, meaning "not" and *fant*, meaning "to talk." Related word: *infantry*.

Iowa—from the Dakota *ayuba*, meaning "the sleepy ones."

January—derived from the Latin *Januarius*—*janus* meaning "gate" or specifically, the two-faced god of gates. As the first month of the Ancient Roman calendar (added by the second king of Rome around 700 B.C.E.), January sees the end of the old year and begins the new year.

Jeep—from the abbreviation for the all-purpose vehicle developed for the military. The "general purpose" vehicle was nicknamed *g.p.*, which was shortened into one syllable.

July—originally *Quintilis*, from the Latin *quintus*, meaning "fifth," as it was the fifth month on the Ancient Roman calendar. In 44 B.C.E., the month was renamed *Julius* to honor Gaius Julius Caesar (born during the month). By Middle English, it had changed to *July*.

June—honored the Roman goddess *Junius*. From the Latin *Junius*, the Old English changed it to *June* in the 14th century.

Kansas—from "Kansa" meaning Sioux people.

Kentucky—from the Iroquois *kenta-ke*, meaning "meadowlands."

kindergarten—invented in 1840. German word literally meaning "a children's garden." Friedrich Froebel, who founded the kindergarten system, was an educator who did research and was committed to the theory of early childhood education.

language—from the Middle English *langage*, meaning "tongue." Related words: *linguist*, *linguine*.

leotard—created by Jules Leotard, a 19th century trapeze performer who needed a more comfortable outfit in which to perform.

leprechaun—derived from the Irish Gaelic *leipreachan* or *luprachan*, *lu* meaning "small" and *corpan* meaning "body."

Louisiana—named for King Louis XIV of France.

lunch—from the Old English *lunshin,* meaning "a lump of food." *Schench* at that time meant "a drink." The two words were combined to mean a lump of food with drink. Then *luncheon* was shortened to *lunch. Breakfast* means "break the fast," *supper* means "to sup," and *dinner* was from the French *diner,* meaning "to dine."

macaroni—borrowed from Italians, derived from the Greek *makaria,* meaning "blessed." In Greece this was a barley and broth cake, the Italians used it to mean any mixture, especially since their pasta had so many different sauces.

Maine—probably named for the region in France from which some of the first explorers came.

manila—from the Filipino word *manila,* meaning "hemp," which is used to make paper.

map—from the Latin *mappa* meaning "loincloth" (the first maps were drawn on loincloths), which changed to *mundi,* meaning "sheet of the world." Related word: *napkin.*

marathon—from the ancient Greek town of Marathon. In 490 B.C.E., against great odds, the Athenians defeated the Persians on the plains of Marathon. Pheidippides ran the grueling 25 miles back to Athens to deliver the great news. He entered the city gates, yelled "Nike" (victory), and dropped dead. When the first modern Olympics were held in Athens in 1896, the 25-mile dash was recreated. The current distance, 26 miles and 385 yards, became the standard after the 1908 Olympics in London. The extra distance was added so that the race could end in front of the Royal box in the stadium.

March—from the Latin *Martius* or *Mars,* who was first the god of agriculture and then the god of war. This was originally the first month of the ancient Roman calendar. The word *Martius* traveled to the Old French as *March* at the beginning of the 13th century.

marshmallow—derived from the food made 2,000 years ago from the root of the Mediterranean *malua* plant. Because it grew in the marsh, the food became known as *marishmalua,* or *marshmallow* in English.

Maryland—first spelled *Marieland,* named for Henrietta Maria, the wife of Charles the II of England.

Massachusetts—from the Algonquin phrase *mass adchu-ceuck,* meaning "big hills people."

mathematics—from the Greek *math,* meaning "learning," or *mat,* meaning "to act" or "to move."

May—probably named for the mother of Mercury, *Maia.* Old French changed the name to *Mai,* then the word changed to *May* in Middle English.

meat—from the Old English *mete,* which came from the old Germanic *med,* meaning "to be fat." At the time, *mete* refered to any kind of food, but during the 15th century, it began to be used to refer to the flesh of animals.

meter—from the Latin *metrum,* Greek *metron,* and Old French *metre,* meaning "to measure." Related words: *metric, pentameter.*

meteor—from the Greek *meteor,* meaning "high in the air" and the Latin *meteorum,* meaning "thing in the heaven above."

metropolitan—from the Latin *metropolitanus* and the Greek *metropolis,* meaning "mother city."

Michigan—What we now call Lake Michigan impressed the Chippewa, who referred to this region as *mica gama,* meaning "big water."

Minnesota—from the Dakota *Minisota,* meaning "white water."

Mississippi—from the Chippewa *mici sipi,* meaning "big river."

Missouri—named for the people living along its river, called Oumissouri meaning "town of large canoes."

modern—from the Latin *modernus,* meaning "just now."

monarch—from the Greek *monarches, monos* meaning "alone" and *arches* meaning "ruler."

Montana—Spanish, meaning "land mountains."

Morse code—named after Samuel Morse, who invented the electronic dot and dash system of communication.

nausea—from the Latin *nausea* and Greek *nausia. Nau* meaning "ship," it was used to describe the feeling of sickness one gets from being on a ship. Related word: *nautical.*

Nebraska—the Platte River in southern Nebraska was referred to by the Omaha Indians as *ni bthaska,* meaning "broad river."

Nevada—this unique name is Spanish and means "snow." Although the vast majority of the state rarely sees snow, the early Spanish explorers were impressed by what are now called the Sierra Nevada mountains in the northern part of the state.

New Hampshire—In 1622, the Council for New England gave Captain John Mason this large tract of land. He named it after his home, Hampshire County in England.

New Jersey—originally part of New Netherland, which was occupied by the Dutch. The British took over this area, it was renamed for an island off the coast of England, which was the home of James, Duke of York, who was granted this land by his brother, Charles II, the King of England.

New Mexico—Spanish explorers coming from Mexican settlements called this area *Nuevo Mexico.*

New York—This region originally was part of New Netherland, until the British occupation, when it was renamed for the Duke of York.

nickname—from the Middle English *eek,* meaning "other." *Eekname,* meaning "another name," changed to *nickname* over time.

North Carolina—from the Latin form of *Charles* (Carolus), named for King Charles II.

North Dakota—from the Sioux *Dakota,* meaning "friend."

November—originally the ninth month, thus named *novem,* meaning "nine." This became *Novembre* in the Old French and Middle English. Latin influenced the spelling of its current form.

October—originally the eighth month, thus named *octo*, meaning "eight." This became *Octobre* in the Old French and Middle English. Latin influenced the spelling of its current form.

Ohio—from the Iroquois *oheo*, meaning "beautiful water."

Oklahoma—from two Choctaw words: *okla*, meaning "people" and *homa*, meaning "red."

onion—from the Latin *unionem*, meaning "one." An onion has many layers that unite to make one sphere.

orange—a Middle English word from the Sanskrit *naranga*, meaning "fragrant."

orangutan—from the Malay *orang*, meaning "man" and *utan* meaning "forest."

Oregon—has two possible sources. One is the Algonquin *wauregan*, meaning "water" or the French Canadian *ouragan*, meaning "hurricane."

patriot—from the Latin *patriota* and the Greek *patriotes*, meaning "of one's father" or "characteristics of one's forefathers."

Pennsylvania—from the Latin *sylvania*, meaning "wooded land." The land was chosen by William Penn so the King of England added the *Penn*, thus making a word that means "Penn's wooded land."

philanthropy—from the Latin and Greek *philanthropia*, with *phil* meaning "loving" and *anthropos* meaning "man."

Piedmont—from the Latin *ped*, meaning "foot" and *mont* meaning "mountain" or "hill." Related words: *pedestrian, Pied Piper, podiatrist.*

piggy bank—in the 1400s, household pots and dishes in England were made of a cheap clay called *pygg*. Housewives would store extra coins in the these *pyggy jars*. They became known as *pygg banks*. Over the next 300 years, pygg was no longer a commonly used material, but the English potters still made *piggy banks*, shaped like pigs.

pilgrim—from the Latin *peregrinus*, meaning "foreigner" or "being abroad."

pioneer—from the Latin *pedon*, meaning "foot" and the French *peonier*, meaning "foot soldier."

port—from the Latin *portus*, meaning "door," "entrance," or "gate." The left side of the boat was typically next to the dock, so this was where one would enter the boat. Today the left side of the ship is still referred to as the port side.

Popsicle—in 1923, Frank Epperson froze soda pop in seven fruit flavors and called them *Epsicles*. This later was changed to *popsicle*.

president—from the Latin *praesideo*, meaning "to protect" or "to sit in front of."

protect—from the Latin *pro*, meaning "on behalf of" and *tect*, meaning "to cover."

purple—from the Middle English *purpel* and the Latin *purpura* for the color.

question—from the Latin *quaerere*, meaning "to seek" or "to ask." Related word: *request.*

recess—from the Latin *recessus,* meaning "to withdraw" or "to recede."

Rhode Island—first called the Isle of Rhodes, from the Dutch meaning red clay island.

ritzy—from the elegant Ritz Carlton Hotel.

rodeo—invented in 1834. Taken from the Spanish verb *rodear,* meaning "to go around," from the Latin *rota,* meaning "wheel."

salad—from the Latin *sal,* meaning "salt" and Middle French *salade,* meaning "salted." The first salads were made of fresh items that were preserved in a salted mixture.

salary—also comes from *sal* because, in Roman times, soldiers were paid so they could buy salt, a necessary but expensive commodity. *Salary*, then, was the monetary means to purchase the necessary salt. The phrase "worth your salt" also comes from this, as does "salt of the earth."

sandwich—named after the Fourth Earl of Sandwich, an English nobleman who lived in the 1700s. The sandwich was created so that the Earl did not have to interrupt his card game…he simply ate his bread and meat together.

school—originated from Greek *schole,* meaning "leisure." Only the man of leisure had time to contemplate, lecture, and discuss. Around 30 B.C.E., the word changed to mean "a place of learning." The Romans borrowed it as *schola,* to use in the same way. Christian missionaries borrowed it and changed it to *scole,* then *school.*

science—from the Latin *sci,* meaning "to know."

senate—from the Latin *senex,* meaning "an old man." In Rome, a *senate* was a council of old men. Related word: *senile.*

sideburns—named for the American Civil War Union General Ambrose Everett Burnside, who was known for his bushy side whiskers. When these became popular, an anagram of his name changed it to its current form.

September—was originally the seventh month, thus named *septem,* which means "seven." This became *septembre* in the Old French and Middle English. Latin influenced the spelling of its current form.

sketch—derived from the Dutch *schets,* borrowed from the Italian *schizzo* (to splash) and from the Latin *schedium* (an extemporaneous poem), all from the Greek *schedios,* meaning "made off-hand."

slogan—from the Celtic *sluagh,* meaning "host," "crowd," "multitude." This, combined with the Gaelic *gairm,* meaning "shout" or "cry," first appeared in Scottish English as *slughorne, sloghorne,* or *slogurn.* This word was eventually used to describe any word or phrase that expressed an attitude, goal, or position.

soccer—form of the abbreviation for Association (assoc). The soccer game we know in the United States was called Association Football in Great Britain and many other countries. When the game was brought here, we already had a sport called football, so the abbreviation was used to create a new word.

solve—from the Latin *solvere,* meaning "to unfasten" or "to free."

somersault—from the Latin *sober,* meaning "above" and *saut,* meaning "to leap."

South Carolina—from the Latin form of *Charles (Carolus)*; named for King Charles II.

South Dakota—from the Sioux *dakota,* meaning "friend."

spaghetti—origin is unknown, but the word is the plural of the Italian *spago,* meaning "string."

spirit—from the Latin *esprit* or *spiritus,* meaning "breath." Related word: *respiration.*

starboard—from the Old English *steorbor* or *steor,* meaning "rudder" or "the steering oar" and *bor,* meaning "a side." In the early ships, the steering mechanism was on the right-hand side of the ship.

surgery—from the Latin *chirurgia* and the Greek *kheirourgia,* both meaning "hand work."

sympathy—from the Latin *sym* meaning "together" and *path* meaning "feeling."

teacher—from the Old English *tacen,* meaning "to show" or "to instruct."

teddy bear—from the nickname for President Theodore Roosevelt. Although he liked to hunt big game, a newspaper cartoon showed him sparing the life of a bear cub. A toy company made a toy bear cub and named it after him.

Tennessee—from the name of a Cherokee settlement called *Tinnase* in what is now the state.

test—from the Latin *testum,* which was a general term for an earthen vessel. During the Middle Ages, the word descended through the French language to mean a specific type of vessel used to measure precious metals. When the vessel was heated, impure materials were absorbed and what remained was pure silver or gold. In time, the word began to be used figuratively for any evaluation or examination, and eventually changed to its current form, *test.*

Texas—originated from the Caddo word *texia,* meaning "friend." The Spanish used the word *tejas,* meaning "ally" or "friend." A combination of the two gave us the current spelling.

tobacco—started in the West Indies and traveled to Spain as *tabaco,* which was the name of the pipe from which it was smoked.

tulip—derived from the Turkish *tulbend* and then the French *tulipan,* both meaning "turban." The turban-like appearance of this flower gives it its name.

tutu—meaning "ballet skirt," alteration of the French *cucu* meaning "rear end" or "bottom."

typhoon—from the Chinese *tai fung,* meaning "big wind" and used to describe a type of storm in the China seas or near the Philippines. It was then altered due to its similarity in spelling to the Greek *typhon,* meaning "violent wind."

Utah—from the Ute, meaning "land of the Ute people."

value—from the Latin *valere,* meaning "to be strong" or "to have worth."

verb—Latin, meaning "word." Related words: *verbose, verbal, verbiage, proverb.*

Vermont—first called New Connecticut, and later named by French explorers using the words *vert,* meaning "green" and *mont,* meaning "mountain."

Virginia—named for Queen Elizabeth I, who was known as the Virgin Queen. Virginia was also a land that was untouched by Europeans, and therefore "virgin" land.

volt—named for Alessandro Volta, who developed the theory of current electricity.

volunteer—from Latin *voluntarius,* meaning "to wish" or "to will."

war—from the Angl-Norman or Old French *werre,* meaning "confusion," "discord," or "strife." Related words: *warrior, warfare.*

warden—from the Old English *weardian,* meaning "to nurse" or "to look after."

Washington—originates in Anglo-Saxon *wasch,* meaning "seaside" or "water." The state was named for George Washington.

West Virginia—became a separate state to remain a part of the Union during the Civil War. Originally was a part of Virginia.

white—from the Old English *hwit,* meaning "brightness" or "light."

window—when Norse carpenters built homes, they left a hole or "eye" in the roof to allow smoke to escape. Wind often blew through this hole and it became known as *vindr auga,* meaning "wind eye." English builders modified the Norse word when they borrowed it, changing it to *window.*

Wisconsin—from the Ojibwa Wishkonsing, meaning "place of the beaver."

write—from the Old English *writan,* meaning "to scratch," "to draw," or "to engrave."

Wyoming—from the Algonquin *weam-ing,* meaning "big flat lands."

Xerox—derived from the Greek *xeros,* meaning "dry."

yellow—from the Old English *geolu,* meaning "the color of gold."

yoga—from the Sanskrit *yuga,* meaning "union" or "to join."

zero—from the Arabic *sifr* and Middle Latin *zephirum,* meaning "empty."

zipper—you might be calling this the "slide fastener" if the B.F. Goodrich company hadn't decided to give their 1925 invention a more interesting name. The inventors wanted to find a way to describe the speed and sound of this new invention, so *zip* was selected and the *-er* suffix added.

zoo—an abbreviated form of *zoological gardens,* from the New Latin *zoologia,* meaning "animals."

ACRONYMS

(a word created from the first letter of each word of a phrase)

AWOL—Absent Without Leave

EPCOT—Experimental Prototype Community Of Tomorrow

FedEx—FEDeral EXpress

LASER—Light Amplification by Stimulated Emission of Radiation

LEGO—Leg Godt, Danish for "play well," used by the Danish toy company for its name and product.

METRO—METROpolitan Railway

NABISCO—NAtional BIScuit COmpany

NASA—National Aeronautics and Space Administration

OPEC—Organization of Petroleum Exporting Countries

PAKISTAN—Punjab, Afghan border states, Kashmir, Sind, BaluchisTAN

PIN—Personal Identification Number

POSH—Port Out, Starboard Home, having to do with the best cabins aboard ship (due to the position of the sun) as passengers traveled between England and India.

RADAR—RAdio Detecting And Ranging

RAM—Random Access Memory

ROM—Read Only Memory

SCUBA—Self-Contained Underwater Breathing Apparatus.

SNAFU—Situation Normal All Fouled Up

SONAR—SOund Navigation And Ranging

TEFLON—TEtraFLOroethylene resiN

UNICEF—United Nations International Children's Emergency Fund

ZIP code—Zone Improvement Plan

The Spelling List and Word Study Resource Book · Scholastic Professional Books

PORTMANTEAUS

(A portmanteau is a large leather suitcase that opens into two compartments, but it is also used to describe a word created by blending two or more other words—and their meanings. Lewis Carroll coined this use of the word.)

aerosol: aero + solution

bash: bang + smash

blurt: blow + spurt

brash: bold + rash

breathalyzer: breath + analyzer

brunch: breakfast + lunch

camcorder: camera + recorder

cellophane: cellulose + diaphane

charbroil: charcoal + broil

chortle: chuckle + snort

chump: chunk + lump

clink: click + clank

cosmonaut: comos + astronaut

con man: confidence + man

ditsy: dizzy + dotty

doodle: dodder + toddle

dumbfound: dumb + confound

Ebonics: ebony + phonics

electrocute: electric + execute

Eurail Pass: European + railway + pass

farewell: fare + ye + well

flabbergast: flap + aghast

flare: flame + glare

flaunt: flout + vaunt

flop: flap + drop

flurry: flutter + hurry

fortnight: fourteen + night

Gestapo: gheime + staatpolize (German state police)

gimp: game + limp

glimmer: gleam + shimmer

glob: globe + blob

glop: goo + slop

good-bye: God + be (with) + ye

goon: gorilla + baboon

happenstance: happen + circumstance

heliport: helicopter + airport

humongous: huge + tremendous

intercom: internal + communication

Internet: international + network

modem: modulator + demodulator

moped: motor + pedal

motel: motor + hotel

motorcade: motor + cavalcade

Muppet: marionette + puppet

pang: pain + sting

paratrooper: parachute + trooper

prissy: prim + sissy

prod: poke + rod

pulsar: pulsating + star

rubbage: rubbish + garbage

rustle: rush + hustle

sci-fi: science + fiction

scrawl: scribble + sprawl

scrunch: squeeze + crunch

sitcom: situation + comedy

slang: slovenly + language

slather: slap + lather

smog: smoke + fog

splotch: spot + blotch

snazzy: snap + jazzy

squawk: squall + squeak

squiggle: squirm + wiggle

spork: spoon + fork

swipe: sweep + wipe

telecast: television + broadcast

telethon: television + marathon

travelogue: travel + monologue

twirl: twist + whirl

Chapter 3
Idioms: 50 Fascinating Stories to Share With Students

Man does not live by words alone,
despite the fact that sometimes he has to eat them.
—Adlai E. Stevenson Jr. (1900–1965)

In the above quote, Adlai Stevenson used the idiom *eat your words*, which means we sometimes have to reconsider or apologize for something we said. This particular idiom reaches as far back as 1370 C.E. when the Pope of the Catholic Church sent two emissaries bearing a parchment to inform Bernardo Viscounti of his excommunication from the church. Enraged, Viscounti made the emissaries eat the parchment, literally eating their words. In our research we found that many idioms could be traced back to such literal definitions; then, over time, they evolved to be the colloquialism that we use today.

The English language has more than 15,000 idioms. Many have been translated into other languages and many languages have their own, unique phrases that have meanings relative to their culture. The Greek and Latin word *idioma* means peculiar. *Webster's Third New International Dictionary* defines an idiom as "the language proper or peculiar to a people or to a district, community or class" (p.1123). Linguists and lexicographers often debate a phrase's origin, for in some cases the exact verifiable history is lost, which is not surprising considering that words morph over time through many languages. Idioms may use obscure words that are rarely used alone, but meaningful when used in the idiom. For example, "Giving someone a wide berth," means to give him or her space, but we rarely use the word *berth* any more, which refers to the space to dock a boat, or the sleeping space on trains and steamships. Since few of us travel that way today, the word is fairly obsolete, but understandable when used in an idiom.

Spending curriculum time on idioms isn't just about stirring students' curiosity—idioms are an important part of the English language. They are most frequently spoken and less frequently written. Learning idioms is particularly important to the English Language Learners (ELL or ESL) in our classrooms who need help in understanding colloquial speech.

One inviting way to begin an introduction to idioms is to share some examples with students and ask them to guess how the phrase started. Once they have offered ideas, they will be eager to learn the real story. Ask students to keep track of idioms they read in their literature (think Amelia Bedelia who takes idioms literally—remember when she got out paper and pencil to "draw the curtains?") or they hear people say in everyday conversation. Begin a collection of these on a bulletin board or flip chart. Following is a selection of idioms students might commonly hear or ones we believe are appropriate when integrated into various areas of the curriculum.

All over but the shouting (a clear decision had been made prior to the conclusion). In past centuries, English common law allowed for local issues to be decided using a voice vote. A specified day and time was posted and citizens gathered to express their views by shouting. It was not unusual, however, for the outcome of the ballot or issue at hand to have been decided beforehand. In such case, the politics of that time used the term "all over but the shouting" to signify that they would still go through the motions of having a public meeting.

Apple of my eye (favorite or pet). As far back as the 9th century, the pupil of the eye was considered an important spot of our anatomy. The pupil is apple shaped, and because it is so vital to life, anything precious (such as loved ones) was called the apple of their eye.

Baker's dozen (thirteen). In 1266, England regulated standard quantities of baked goods. Bakers would overcompensate by including an extra loaf to be sure they met the law.

Be in the hole (to owe money). In the 1800s, when a poker player won, a certain amount of the money won had to go to the "house," or the place where the game was played. There was a slot in the table for this money, and winners of each hand were required to put money "in the hole."

Between the devil and the deep blue sea (trapped between equally difficult situations). A nautical term, the "devil" was the seam on a wooden sailing ship, close to the water. It was an awkward place, and sailors who were chosen to caulk the devil quite literally found themselves between the devil and the deep blue sea.

Big wig (a person of authority). During the 17th and 18th centuries, English aristocrats, judges, and clerics wore full-length wigs. The more important the person was, the bigger the wig he wore.

Bite off more than you can chew (attempting to manage more than one is able to). Originated in America, this became a popular idiom during the Civil War when a plug of tobacco was passed around and a greedy man might bite off more tobacco than he could chew.

Blue blood (of nobility, or socially prominent). When the Moors invaded Spain, the Spanish aristocrats had such fair skin that their veins could be seen through the skin, and the Moors used this phrase to refer to the aristocrats. These blue veins were thus associated with royalty.

Bone to pick (a disagreement to address). Similar idioms can be found in many cultures. The same idea in German translates into "a bird to pluck," and in French it's "a knot to pick." This expression originates in Ancient Rome, where a difficult situation was described as "a pebble to throw."

Bury the hatchet (settle differences). Native Americans would not declare peace between warring tribes until all of the warriors had literally buried their hatchets. If the peace did not last, the tomahawks were unearthed.

By and by (in a little while, eventually). Used for many centuries, originally this phrase was written *bi and bi*, which meant "neatly ordered" or "in place." Eventually it meant "one by one;" in other words, things must happen in order.

By and large (generally speaking). This is a combination of two old sailing terms. *By* meant "to be against the wind" and *large* meant "with the wind." In nautical terms, this suggested that the wind could be before the beam or after the beam, but the average wind was needed to sail.

Chew the fat (sit around and talk). Sailors enjoyed salt pork, but when supplies ran low they were forced to chew the layer of fat that was left. This chewing took time, so the sailors would engage in conversation while they "chewed the fat."

Chip on your shoulder (a bad attitude caused by a lingering sense of inferiority). This expression originated in America at a time when placing a chip of wood on one's shoulder was a challenge and an invitation to fight.

Chips are down (situation has a reached a moment of truth). In gambling, when the chips are down, all the bets have been placed but the outcome of the game is still unknown.

Climb into bed (go to bed for the night). In Colonial times, people were much shorter than they are today. Men were about 5 feet 2 inches to 5 feet 7 inches; women were generally less than 5 feet tall. Beds were high off the floor to allow for the "slop pot" (bed pan). So people had to literally climb to get into their beds.

Cross your fingers (to hope for luck). Slaves in America originated this phrase. Crossing one's fingers was an easy, and perhaps discrete, way to make the sign of the cross to protect themselves from the tricks of the devil.

Couch potato (an idle or lazy person). This is a fairly new idiom, which describes a person who vegetates in front of the television, lounging on a couch. "Potato" was probably chosen by whomever coined the phrase because it is a bland, round vegetable.

Flash in the pan (a moment of brilliance that does not last). This refers to the misfiring of a flintlock gun. When the flint hit the hammer, a spark was fired from the pan, which held the gunpowder. This explosion caused the musket ball to fire incorrectly. The result was nothing more than a flash in the gunpowder pan.

Getting up on the wrong side of the bed (having a bad day). This expression originated during Roman times. Romans believed that evil spirits dwelled on the left side of the bed. Arising and setting foot on the left side of the bed would cause the evil spirits to affect the person throughout the day.

Go AWOL (leaving without permission, absent without leave). Originated during the Civil War, this term described soldiers who left their regiment without permission. This was carried on and used in World War I, World War II, and today.

Go whole hog (go the whole way). The prevailing theory on this idiom starts with the fact that, in the 18th and 19th century, an Irish shilling was called a *hog*. This was equivalent to an American ten-cent piece. A person willing to spend the entire shilling, therefore, went "whole hog."

Hem and haw (to express uncertainty). As early as the 1400s, writings refer to the "humys" (hums) and "hays" (has or haws) of men who hesitated when speaking. Shakespeare described it as "hum and ha," reflecting the sounds we make when we clear our throats to speak.

His name is mud (he has a bad reputation). When John Wilkes Booth assassinated President Abraham Lincoln on April 14, 1865, he jumped from the theater balcony to the stage below, breaking his leg. He rode out to the country, where he stopped at Dr. Samuel Mudd's home seeking medical attention. Dr. Mudd set his leg, not knowing about the events that had just occurred. Later, Dr. Mudd was arrested as an accomplice. He was tried and sentenced to life in prison. President Andrew Johnson pardoned Mudd in 1869 after he helped treat victims of a yellow fever outbreak in the prison. Public sentiment still held that he had played some part in what happened, however, and he was not forgiven. In the 1970s, the Mudd family was finally able to have Dr. Mudd officially declared innocent, but the idiom has stayed with us.

In the nick of time (just in time). Until 1826, before the invention of timepieces, officials at sporting events would keep track of time using a device called a *nick-stick*. Intervals of time were nicked into a stick.

Knuckle down (to concentrate fully on a task at hand). Ancient marbles were actually small stones. In the 1500s, Dutch artisans discovered how to make small balls out of porcelain. Within the next century, the game of marbles became a favorite of both children and adults. One of the rules of the game was that marbles had to be placed across the center of a ring in the dirt. When a player used the shooter marble to shoot the opponent's marbles out of the ring, he had to keep one knuckle down until he released the marble. This took extreme concentration in order to make a precise shot.

Let the cat out of the bag (to tell a secret). This idiom is related to the idiom **pig in a poke** (buying something you thought was valuable, but it was not). In England, salesmen would travel with country fairs and they were often not very honest. A *poc* was a Celtic word meaning "sack," which eventually became *poke*, so you bought "pigs in a poke"—or a litter of small pigs in a sack. If an unassuming customer did not look in the sack until arriving home, he might find kittens instead of pigs. Smart buyers would therefore open the bag to "let the cat out," if indeed they were being cheated.

Limelight (center of attention) In the early 1800s, Thomas Drummond discovered that when calcium oxide (lime) is heated, it gives off a glaring white light. This "limelight" was used in lighthouses and later in theaters.

Lock, stock, and barrel (the whole thing, total and complete). Originally a lock, a stock, and a barrel were the three main parts of a gun. Therefore, having something lock, stock, and barrel means nothing has been omitted.

Mend fences (to make up). During the presidential campaign of 1880, John Sherman, an Ohio senator, left Washington, D.C., to return to his farm in Mansfield, Ohio. When a rumor circulated that he had returned to his farm to secretly meet with backers so that he could become a presidential candidate, a reporter boldly entered Sherman's property, only to discover Sherman and a Colonel Moulton mending a fence. The reporter, hoping to get the inside story, asked Sherman what he was doing. He replied, "mending fences" so as not to disclose what he was really doing, which was making amends with potential backers for his presidential campaign.

Nest egg (savings for the future). When chickens were domesticated, farmers found that hens were more likely to lay eggs if other eggs were already in the nest. Clever farmers placed a small porcelain egg in the nest. The result was extra eggs, thus more profit. The extra money was set aside and called a nest egg.

Once in a blue moon (very rarely). The illusion of a blue moon really does occur, but is very rare. Blue moons are caused by dust particles or forest fires that cause the Earth's view of the moon to seem to have a blue halo.

Over a barrel (in a compromising position). Placing a person face down over a barrel used to be a means of resuscitation. The barrel would be gently rolled in an attempt to bring the drowned or choking person back to life. This person was at the mercy of those assisting him.

Pass the buck (pass on a job or responsibility). This is an old card-playing phrase. The buck was a marker to show which player was the dealer. At the end of the hand, the responsibility of dealing was passed to the next person.

Pull someone's leg (to tease someone or toy with them). This practice still occurs: Two muggers working together choose a victim; one trips her then the others takes her valuables. Over centuries, industrious robbers invented a special walking stick with a curved end that was perfect for hooking and pulling the victim's leg.

Pull up stakes (to move, change locations). In Colonial times, when a settler was dissatisfied with his plot of land, he could pull up the stakes that marked the boundaries of his property and move elsewhere.

Pull the wool over your eyes (to deceive). (See big wigs). The large wigs worn by 16th- and 17th-century judges were often made of wool. A lawyer who felt he had tricked a judge into ruling in his favor would brag that he had "pulled the wool" over the judge's eyes.

Seventh heaven (sheer delight). Muslims believe there are seven heavens, each made of precious stones. The seventh is the most precious and represents the level of spiritual ecstasy.

Skeletons in the closet (something to hide). In the early 1800s, it was illegal for physicians to dissect bodies. Due to the high demand for bodies, some doctors paid grave robbers to dig up corpses to be used for medical use. Because this practice was not legal, the doctors hid the skeletons in a cupboard or closet.

Sleep tight (sleep well). In Colonial times, mattresses were held in bed frames with a criss crossing of ropes. These needed to be tightened occasionally, or the mattress would sag, causing an uncomfortable night's sleep.

Something up his sleeve (a deceitful plan). During the 15th century, gentlemen's garments did not have pockets. Important items were instead hung from a belt. A clever tailor found that by making the sleeves fuller between the elbow and the wrist, fashionable men could tuck various items in these new "pockets." This novel idea took off and sleeves eventually became large enough to drape on the ground. Henry VIII put an end to this fashion trend, but the term remained.

Start from scratch (start at the very beginning). Originally the starting point of any race was a line scratched in the earth, named "the scratch." So to begin a horse race, for instance, the horses would start from the scratch. (**Toe the line**, meaning to do your part, also comes from races. All runners had to keep their toe on the starting line at the outset of the race.)

The third degree (intense interrogation). This term was originally associated with the lodge of Free Masons. The third degree was the final stage of proficiency in order to attain the title of Master Mason. Reaching the third degree was a secret, severe, and difficult test of a man's ability.

To boot (in addition, as well). This term comes from the Anglo Saxon word *bot*, which meant to have the advantage, profit, or everything needed. Although the word *bot* is no longer used, the idiom "to boot" took on the meaning.

Turncoat (a traitor). While many specific stories exist, we *do* know that the common theme in all of these stories is a reversible coat in which one could quickly hide their allegiance or change allegiances. Soldiers running from battle and wishing to hide who they were or politicians living between two warring countries and afraid to side with just one were known to reverse their coats.

Under the weather (sick). On ships, when the weather started getting rough, the sailors would go below deck to try to avoid getting sick. These seamen quite literally were going under the weather.

Warts and all (with all flaws). Oliver Cromwell, a Puritan, commissioned Sir Peter Lely to paint his portrait. The practice of the time was to make rich and powerful people look perfect in portraits, but Cromwell insisted that Lely paint him "warts and all."

White-collar worker (a professional person). A recent idiom, this saying began in World War I to identify workers by their clothing. So a "black-coated worker" was a cleric, a "white-collar worker" was in a respected managerial profession, and a "blue-collar" worker was a laborer.

Chapter 4
Organized Word Lists: A Handy Resource for Spelling Instruction

Teachers open the door.
You enter by yourself.
—Chinese Proverb

Learning to spell is a developmental process. This process entails learning that continuously builds on prior knowledge of letters, sounds and words. During a particular phase of learning there are word features that are most appropriate for instruction that provide a foundation for students' knowledge about the conventions of spelling. If you would like to find out more about the phases of spelling development, we encourage you to look at our companion book, *Teaching and Assessing Spelling* (Fresch & Wheaton, 2002). The book also contains a variety of assessments to identify your students' needs and give direction to your spelling instruction.

The word lists compiled for you are organized by word features. The words become progressively more complex. We have grouped the lists in grade level spans to help you determine what might be appropriate for your students' and to help you enhance any spelling program you are currently using. We urge you to focus on your students' spelling needs rather than on grade-leveled lists. Our lists differ from any other published lists because the intention is not memorization of whole words. Instead, the intent is to study words with a focus on particular features. Why? Research indicates that a student's growing knowledge about a feature will carry into their independent writing as their understanding expands to inform their predictions of conventional spellings. Spelling instruction based on a memorization model, on the other hand, has little carry over to independent writing. The goal of any spelling instruction must be to support a student's ability to be an autonomous writer.

The words we have selected came from a number of research-based resources. We have selected word families (rimes), high-frequency words, content-related words, and a variety of vocabulary from grade-leveled texts. Please feel free to add your own examples.

Short Vowels—a

Grades K/1
add
am
an
and
as
ask
at
back
bad
bag
bat
bath
black
can
cap
cat
clap
dad
fan
fat
flag
flat
glad
had
has
hat
have
jam
lap
mad
man
map
mat
pad
pal
pan
pat
plan
ran

rat
sad
sand
sat
slap
snap
tag
tan
tap
than
that
trap

Grades 1/2
ant
ask
ban
bang
brag
clam
class
cram
fact
fast
flap
gas
grab
half
hand
happy
having
lamp
land
last
match
math
nap
pants
past
patch

path
rag
sap

Grades 2/3
after
answer
apple
attach
attack
backpack
began
brat
can't
captain
catch
chapter
damp
dance
draft
drag
gnat
hatch
icepack
lack
mask
matter
newscast
rabbit
rack
ranch
scab
snap
stab
swam
task
that's
wax

Grade 3/4
absent
actor
address
adventure
afternoon
alphabet
another
Atlantic
attract
avenue
baggage
banner
basket
batch
brass
cabbage
camping
canyon
capacity
catcher
classroom
craft
cramp
draft
dragon
fact
factory
famine
fraction
galaxy
gallon
gases
gather
glance
grabbed
grandfather
grandmother
graph
grass

haystack
hazard
January
kilogram
lasting
macaroni
magnetic
mammal
math
napkin
negative
organ
passage
pathway
pattern
planet
raccoon
prance
quack
sack
Saturn
scramble
scrap
scrapbook
scratch
shadow
shampoo
smash
splashing
splatter
stack
standing
strand
subtract
taxes
taxi
tractor
traffic
trapeze
unhappy

Short Vowels—e

Grades K/1

bed
beg
bell
bet
egg
end
fed
fell
get
hen
jet
leg
let
men
met
net
pen
pet
red
sell
set
sled
tell
ten
web
wet
yes
yet

Grades 1/2

best
deck
den
end
left

less
neck
peck
rest
said
shelf
shell
smell
sped
spell
step
tent
them
then
well
went
when
yell

Grades 2/3

been
better
bread
cent
chest
dead
death
desk
dress
edge
elephant
ending
ever
everything
feather
fence

friend
getting
guess
head
kept
lesson
next
read
send
sent
west
yellow

Grades 3/4

arithmetic
bench
blend
breath
breathless
deaf
elbow
envelope
everyone
except
explain
feather
flesh
freckle
fresh
guess
hatchet
health
inches
ketchup
lead
pledge

plenty
skeleton
sketch
slept
smell
special
splendid
splendor
spread
stretch
sweat
sweater
together
twelve
twenty
wealth
weather
whether

Short Vowels—i

Grades K/1
big
bill
bit
crib
did
dig
dip
dish
drip
fill
fin
fish
fit
hid
hill
him
hip
his
hit
if
in
is
it
kick
kid
lick
lid
pick
pig
pin
rich
ship
sit
slid
spin
this
tin
tip
trip
wig

will
win

Grades 1/2
chin
ditch
drill
fist
fix
give
grin
inch
ink
inside
into
itch
kill
king
kiss
lint
list
live
mill
miss
mix
pill
pink
pitch
sick
silly
sing
six
skill
skin
slim
slip
spill
spin
still
swim
thin

thing
trim
twin
wish
witch
with

Grades 2/3
build
built
children
chill
city
clip
crisp
didn't
different
dinner
footprint
gift
important
insist
instead
it's
kidding
knit
lift
little
lived
middle
milk
picture
pitcher
quick
quilt
quit
quiz
riddle
shift
simple
since

sister
split
squid
squish
stiff
swift
thicken
tricked
twig
unhitch
which
winter

Grade 3/4
alligator
Atlantic
auditorium
automatic
chicken
chill
conflict
continent
cricket
didn't
dolphin
fifth
fifty
figure
filling
fishing
fixes
giggle
himself
inches
independence
interesting
investigation
invited
justice
killing
kilogram

kilometer
kitten
liberty
lifting
liquid
listen
magic
magnetic
medicine
million
mixes
multiply
negative
nickels
Pacific
picnic
pitch
positive
pyramid
quilt
quizzes
refill
ribbon
shrimp
since
solid
splinter
stick
switch
thick
thrill
traffic
tripped
uninteresting
unit
village
window
winning
winter
wrist
written

Short Vowels—o

Grades K/1
box
chop
cot
dog
doll
dot
drop
fox
got
hog
hop
hot
job
jog
lot
mom
mop
not
of
on
pop
pot
rob

shop
shot
spot
stop
top

Grades 1/2
crop
dock
drop
frog
gone
lock
log
long
lost
mob
nod
off
ox
rock
rod
sock

Grades 2/3
beyond
block
clock
closet
body
bought
brought
cannot
cost
cough
dock
flock
fossil
fought
knob
knock
knot
moth
notch
odd
pond
rocker
sandbox

slot
soft
thought
unlock

Grades 3/4
blossom
caught
cause
cloth
cost
draw
drawn
frosty
glossary
jaw
law
lawn
o'clock
offer
office
olive
omelet
operation

ostrich
otter
oxygen
paw
problem
promise
sauce
saw
sloppy
smock
smog
somewhat
splotch
straw
strawberry
swat
taught
thoughtful
Washington
watch
watchman

Short Vowels—u

Grades K/1	Grades 1/2			
bud	brush	rung	scrub	lung
bug	bump	rush	scuff	muffin
bun	club	rust	shrub	shrunk
bus	crush	shut	shrug	sponge
but	drum	slug	skull	struggle
come	duck	slum	skunk	stung
cub	dull	such	sprung	sunshine
cup	dump	sum	stuff	thumb
cut	dunk	sung	stump	ugly
fun	dust	sunk	stunk	umbrella
gum	gull	under	trunk	umpire
hug	hump	upon	trust	uncle
jug	hung		unhappy	uncover
love	hunt	**Grades 2/3**	until	underwear
mud	hush	bathtub		unless
mug	jump	bunch		unlock
nut	junk	drug	**Grades 3/4**	upstairs
pup	just	dumb	bubble	
rub	luck	fluff	buck	
rug	lump	glum	bulb	
run	lunch	gruff	butter	
sun	lung	judge	chestnut	
tug	much	number	chunk	
up	must	plum	crumble	
us	plug	plus	cushion	
		punch	ketchup	

Short vowels enclosed by consonant blends/digraphs

a	e	i	o	u
Grades 2/3	**Grades 2/3**	**Grades 2/3**	**Grades 2/3**	**Grades 2/3**
black	blend	brick	block	brush
blast	check	bring	clock	crust
chant		chick	flock	stung
class	**Grades 3/4**	stick		
glass	breath	string	**Grades 3/4**	**Grades 3/4**
grand	bridge	thick	brother	blunt
grass	fresh	thing	chomp	blush
plant	spend	think	cloth	crumb
scratch	spread	trick	frost	flunk
stamp	stretch		knock	grunt
stand	wreck	**Grades 3/4**	shock	plump
		bridge	smock	skunk
Grades 3/4	**Grades 4/5/6**	clicked	stock	slush
blank	breathless	crash	stomp	stump
bland	freckle	crisp	strong	stunt
branch	sketch	drift		thumb
brand	splendor	drink	**Grades 4/5/6**	truck
champ	twenty	print	chalk	trunk
chance		shrink	glossary	trust
clash		splinter	livestock	
clasp		stink	problem	**Grades 4/5/6**
crack		stitch	sponge	brunch
cramp		swift		crunch
crash		swing		shrunk
flash		switch		slump
glance		twist		struck
graph		which		stunt
grasp				
shack		**Grades 4/5/6**		
smash		glimpse		
snack		script		
stamp		snicker		
strand		squint		
track		strict		
trance		twitch		
trash		whiskers		
		whistle		
Grades 4/5/6				
branches				
catcher				
flashlight				
grandchild				
plaster				
scratch				
snatch				

Short vowel in a closed syllable
(a closed syllable begins and ends with a consonant)

Grades 2/3
April
back
began
brat
catch
chin
clip
damp
dock
drag
duck
fish
flock
gift
junk
kick
last
lift
lock
mask
neck
pack
plant
plus
quack
quick
quit
rack
rest
rock
rung
sack
shock
shut
sick
slept

sock
stand
stem
sunk
swam
task
than
that

Grades 3/4
animal
attic
August
bench
bottom
brag
cannot
center
comic
December
fact
February
fifth
follow
fresh
gift
gram
kiss
lettuce
luck
November
office
pencil
plus
pocket
popcorn
raft

recess
September
shell
smell
smock
spaceship
stretch
stung
thumb
tugboat
wagon

Grades 4/5/6
adjective
Africa
agent
bracelet
buttercup
cabin
camel
candle
candy
carpet
castle
catch
celery
cement
central
cinnamon
circus
citizen
council
difficult
doctor
dragon
engine
except

flagship
frantic
gallon
garden
gentle
glance
gorilla
guess
gypsy
happen
helicopter
jiggle
magazine
magnet
metric
necklace
pancake
parcel
picnic
plastic
princess
principal
problem
product
public
scenic
skull
symbol
terrific
ticket
traffic
welcome
zipper

/e/ Marker (final e makes the preceeding vowel long)—long a

Grades 1/2	plane	cage	pane	wave	Grades
ate	rake	case	place	whale	4/5/6
bake	same	cave	plate		ablaze
cake	shape	change	safe	Grades 3/4	amaze
came	take	chase	sale	awake	debate
face	tale	fade	save	flake	locate
game	wake	fake	shade	flame	operate
gate		fame	shake	graze	populate
gave	Grades 2/3	lake	skate	lame	scrape
grade	base	made	snake	maze	
grape	became	make	space	parade	
hate	blame	male	stake	scale	
late	brake	mane	state	trace	
name	brave	page	trade	unsafe	

/e/ Marker (final e makes the preceeding vowel long)—long e

Grades 2/3	scene	centipede	extreme	recede	theme
these		compete	freeze	scheme	trapeze
	Grades	complete	gene	secede	
Grades 3/4	4/5/6	concede	impede	sleeve	
cheese	athlete	concrete	kerosene	sneeze	
eve	breeze	convene	obese	squeeze	
evening	cede	deplete	precede	stampede	

/e/ Marker (final e makes the preceeding vowel long)—long i

Grades 1/2	mine	Grades 2/3	spice	pride	decide
bike	nice	alive	tide	quite	divide
dime	nine	bite	tile	reptile	dynamite
dine	pile	drive	vine	seaside	provide
fine	pine	hive	while	shine	recite
five	pipe	live	wise	spine	scribes
hide	rice	price		tribe	stride
ice	ride	prize	Grades 3/4	write	strike
life	rise	ripe	beside		stripe
like	side	pie	crime	Grades	surprise
line	time	size	define	4/5/6	swine
kite	white	slice	inside	arrive	twice
mice	wide	slide	knife	clockwise	twine
mile		smile	polite	combine	whine

/e/ Marker (final e makes the preceeding vowel long)—long o

Grades 1/2	Grades 2/3	Grades 3/4	Grades 4/5/6
bone	drove	broke	adobe
dome	hole	choke	antelope
home	joke	chose	awoke
hope	nose	globe	bore
those	note	hose	code
	poke	smoke	devote
	rode	spoke	explode
	rose	stone	flagpole
	tadpole	stove	owe
	vote	whole	ozone
	wrote	woke	microphone
	zone		microscope
			notebook
			pole
			slope
			sole
			stroke
			telescope

/e/ Marker (final e makes the preceeding vowel long)—long u

Grades 1/2	Grades 2/3	Grades 3/4	Grades 4/5/6
blue	clue	dune	absolute
use	cube	fuse	acute
	cute	mule	altitude
	glue	mute	amuse
	huge	true	assume
	June	tube	compute
		tune	consume
			flute
			fortune
			fume
			immune
			molecule
			mute
			spruce
			volume

/r/ controlled (the r influences the vowel sound)—ar

Grades 1/2	Grades 2/3	heard	start	scarf	earn
are	ark	heart	started	shark	earth
arm	bark	January	yard	smart	garbage
art	care	jar	yarn	starve	garden
bar	carry	large	year		learn
barn	dark	March		**Grades**	marble
car	fare	mark	**Grades 3/4**	**4/5/6**	pearl
cart	farm	park	barber	burglar	scared
far	February	parka	chart	carton	search
star	hard	part	fare	charge	they're
	hare	smart	March	darling	
	harm	spark	party	early	

/r/ controlled (the r influences the vowel sound)—er

Grades 1/2	feather	paper	Grades 3/4	rubber	either
her	fern	perk	clerk	serve	every
	herd	September	germ	sister	everyone
Grades 2/3	jerk	sister	herb	terms	everything
after	later	summer	however	there	exert
brother	monster	teacher	nerve	where	germ
cover	mother	term	order	winter	hermit
December	never	very	other		pitcher
enter	November	water	perch	**Grades**	several
ever	number	were	perhaps	**4/5/6**	shepherd
farmer	October		person	certain	termite
father	over		pitcher	clover	verse

/r/ controlled (the r influences the vowel sound)—ir

Grades 1/2	Grades 2/3	Grades 3/4	shirt	Grades 4/5/6	squirt
bird	air	birch	skirt	circuit	squirrel
fir	dirt	birth	their	circulate	swirl
first	firm	chirp	thirty	confirm	twirl
girl	hair	circle		dirty	whirl
sir	shirt	circus		giraffe	
stir		flirt		squirm	
third					

/r/ controlled (the r influences the vowel sound)—or

Grades 1/2	force	short	Grades 3/4	score	perform
for	fork	sport	core	torn	porch
or	form	store	corner		record
	fort	storm	forth	Grades 4/5/6	report
Grades 2/3	horse	story	forty		stork
acorn	important	word	morning	editor	sword
born	more	worm	orange	favorite	torch
corn	north	work	order	orchard	worth

/r/ controlled (the r influences the vowel sound)—ur

Grades 1/2	church	purr	Grades 4/5/6	further	turtle
four	churn	purse		hurtle	urge
fur	curb	spur	burglar	jury	
hurt	curl	surf	burst	murmur	
sure	hour	Thursday	concur	occur	
	hurry	turkey	current	picture	
Grades 2/3	nurse	turn	curtain	purpose	
burger	our	under	curve	return	
burn	purple	your	during	sure	

Preconsonant nasals—mp
(sounds made at the back of the nasal cavity)

Grades 2/3	clamp	jump	rump	skimp	thump
bump	clump	lamp		slump	tramp
camp	cramp	limp	**Grades 3/4**	stamp	trump
champ	damp	lump	grump	stomp	tromp
chimp	dump	pump	plump	stump	trumpet
chomp	hump	ramp	shrimp	swamp	

Preconsonant nasals—nch

Grades 2/3	ranch	munch	cinch	hunch	stench
bench		punch	clench	launch	trench
bunch	**Grades 3/4**		clinch	paunch	wrench
inch	branch	**Grades**	drench	quench	unclench
lunch	brunch	**4/5/6**	flinch	scrunch	
pinch	crunch	blanch	French	staunch	

Preconsonant nasals—nd

Grades 2/3	send	ground	tend	command	quicksand
and	wind	hind	trend	compound	rebound
band		hound	understand	correspond	recommend
bend	**Grades 3/4**	lend	unkind	demand	reprimand
bind	around	mend	unwind	extend	respond
bond	behind	mind		firsthand	surround
end	beyond	mound	**Grades**	greyhound	suspend
find	bland	pound	**4/5/6**	husband	wand
found	blend	remind	armband	intend	wound
friend	blind	round	attend	mastermind	
hand	bound	sound	bandstand	offend	
kind	brand	spend	beforehand	offhand	
land	grand	stand	blonde	pretend	
sand	grind	strand	bound	profound	

The Spelling List and Word Study Resource Book · Scholastic Professional Books

Preconsonant nasals—ng

Grades 2/3		Grades 3/4		Grades 4/5/6	
bang	ring	along	strong		sing-along
bring	rung	belong	strung	headstrong	tagalong
gong	sing	clang	stung	high-strung	tong
hung	song	clung	swung	lifelong	unsung
long	sung	flung		oblong	wringer
lung	thing	ringer		prolong	wrong
rang		sprung		prong	wrung

Preconsonant nasals—nk

Grades 2/3				Grades 4/5/6	
bank	sank	blink	plunk		prankster
bunk	sink	chunk	rank	brink	preshrunk
dunk	sunk	clank	shrank	chipmunk	rethink
honk	tank	crank	shrink	gangplank	rinky-dink
ink	thank	drank	shrunk	kerplunk	slink
junk	think	drink	skunk	kink	spank
link	trunk	drunk	slunk	outrank	
mink	wink	flunk	spunk	plank	
pink		frank	stink	plunk	
rink	**Grades 3/4**	Hank	stunk	prank	
	blank	hunk			

Preconsonant nasals—nt

Grades 2/3					
ant	print	faint	appoint	fingerprint	scent
bent	rent	grant	appointment	frequent	servant
cent	sent	grunt	ballpoint	manhunt	splint
dent	spent	newsprint	blueprint	meant	torment
front	tent	paint	cement	merchant	transplant
hint	want	runt	checkpoint	migrant	underwent
hunt	went	tint	compliment	misrepresent	vibrant
invent		urgent	consent	paramount	viewpoint
lent	**Grades 3/4**	vacant	content	participant	
lint	agent		contestant	peasant	
mint	amount	**Grades 4/5/6**	disenchant	peppermint	
pint	current	account	enchant	prevent	
plant	different	accountant	evident	radiant	
	event		experiment	represent	

b
back
ban
bat
beat
beg
bed
best
big
bike
bit
boat
box
boy
bug
bus
but

c
call
can
cap
cat
cell
cent
city
cold
cot
cow
cub
cup
cut

d
dad
date
day
did
dig
dime
dish
do
dog

doll
dot
down
dump

f
fail
fan
fat
fed
feel
feet
fell
fight
fill
fin
fish
fit
fold
for
four
fox
fun

g
game
gate
gave
get
gill
girl
give
go
gold
gone
good
got
gum

h
had
has
hat

have
he
hen
here
hill
him
his
hit
hold
home
hop
hot
how
hug

j
jam
jaw
jet
job
jog
jot
jug
jump
junk
just

k
keep
key
kick
kid
kind
king
kiss
kit
kite

l
lap
late
lay
leg

let
lid
like
line
little
long
look
love
lump

m
mad
made
make
man
mat
me
men
met
mice
milk
mom
mop
much
mud
mug
my

n
name
nap
need
new
nice
night
nine
no
not
now
nut

p
page
pail

pan
pat
pen
pet
pig
pile
poke
pop
pot
put

r
ran
rat
ray
red
rich
ride
right
ring
rob
rod
room
rug
run

s
sad
said
sat
saw
see
seed
shop
sit
so
sold
soon
sun

t
take
tale

tan
tap
tell
ten
time
tip
to
told
too
took
top
tug

v
van
vat
very
vest
vet
visit
vote

w
wag
wake
was
way
we
well
went
wide
will
win
wish
with

y
yank
yap
year
yell
yes
yet

yoke
you
your
yo-yo

z
zap
zero
zest
zing
zip
zoo

Initial consonants blends/digraphs

bl	br	cl	cr	dr	fl
Grades 1/2	**Grades 1/2**	**Grades 1/2**	**Grades 1/2**	**Grades 1/2**	**Grades 1/2**
black	brave	clam	crab	drip	flag
blue	brook	clap	crib	drop	flap
	brother	class	cry	dry	flat
Grades 2/3	brown	clay			flip
blame		clip	**Grades 2/3**	**Grades 2/3**	flow
blaze	**Grades 2/3**	cluck	crack	dress	fly
blew	bread		creep	drill	
block	break	**Grades 2/3**	crook	drive	**Grades 2/3**
blot	breakfast	classroom	crop	drum	flame
	breeze	claw	cross		flea
Grades 3/4	bright	clean		**Grades 3/4**	flew
bleachers	bring	clear	**Grades 3/4**	drank	flight
bleed	broke	clerk	crane	draw	floor
blend	broom	click	crash	dream	flower
blind	brush	cliff	crawl	dresser	flute
blink		clock	creak	drew	
blow	**Grades 3/4**	cloth	cream	dried	**Grades 3/4**
bluff	brace	cloud	creek	drag	flake
	braid	club	creep	droop	flash
Grades 4/5/6	brain		crept	drove	flaw
blade	branch	**Grades 3/4**	crew	drown	fled
blank	brand	claim	cried		fleet
blanket	brass	climb	crisp	**Grades 4/5/6**	flies
blast	breath	close	crossing	draft	flipped
blew	brick	cloud	crowd	dragon	float
blister	bride	clown	crown	drain	flock
blond	bright			drawer	flood
blood	broil	**Grades 4/5/6**	**Grades 4/5/6**	drawn	flour
bloom	brought	clever	cradle	drift	
blossom		closet	craft	drill	**Grades 4/5/6**
blouse	**Grades 4/5/6**	clothes	cramp	drink	flagpole
blur	breathe	clothing	crayon	drive-in	flare
	bridge	cloudy	crazy		flashlight
	broke	clover	cricket		flavor
	brook	clue	crime		fleece
			crosswalk		fleet
			crow		flesh
			crumb		flippers
			crystal		floss
					fluffy

Initial consonants blends/digraphs

fr	gl	gr	pl	pr	sc
Grades 1/2	**Grades 1/2**	**Grades 1/2**	**Grades 1/2**	**Grades 1/2**	**Grades 1/2**
free	glad	grass	plan	prize	scoot
frog	glove	green	plane	pry	
from		grow	plate		**Grades 2/3**
fry	**Grades 2/3**		plow	**Grades 2/3**	scarf
	glass	**Grades 2/3**	plum	pray	scatter
Grades 2/3	glide	grade		present	school
friend	glitter	grain	**Grades 2/3**	pretty	score
front		grand	plain	price	
frost	**Grades 3/4**	grapes	planned	proud	**Grades 3/4**
	glare	gray	play		scare
Grades 3/4	glossy	great	please	**Grades 3/4**	scarecrow
fresh	glow	grew		praise	scene
Friday		groom	**Grades 3/4**	prank	scold
fried	**Grades**		place	president	scout
frill	**4/5/6**	**Grades 3/4**	plank	press	scrape
front	glance	gram	plant	pride	scratch
frosty	glare	grate	playground	prince	scream
	glaze	graze	pledge	princess	screen
Grades	gleam	greasy	plug	produce	scrub
4/5/6	glimpse	greed	plus	proof	
fraction	globe	grey	Pluto	prove	**Grades**
frail	gloom	grill			**4/5/6**
frame	glory	grin	**Grades**	**Grades**	scald
frank	glossary	grind	**4/5/6**	**4/5/6**	scale
freckles	glue	grip	planet	prance	scamper
freedom	glum	ground	plaster	preach	scarce
freeze		growl	plastic	prefer	scent
fright			platter	prefix	schooner
fringe		**Grades**	pleasure	prepare	science
frisky		**4/5/6**	pleat	preserve	scoop
frown		grace	plenty	president	scooter
frozen		graph	pliers	pretend	scour
fruit		gravy	plot	prevent	scowl
		greet	plunge	preview	scribble
		grizzly		problem	script
		groan		promise	scuba
		grocer		propose	scurry
		grouch		protection	
		groundhog		providing	
		group			
		gruff			
		grumpy			

The Spelling List and Word Study Resource Book · Scholastic Professional Books

Initial consonants blends/digraphs

sk	sl	sm	sn	sp	spl
Grades 1/2	**Grades 1/2**	**Grades 1/2**	**Grades 1/2**	**Grades 1/2**	**Grades 1/2**
skip	slap	small	snail	spot	splash
sky	sled	smell	snake	spy	split
	sleep	smile	snap		
Grades 2/3	slid		snip	**Grades 2/3**	**Grades 2/3**
ski	slide	**Grades 2/3**	snow	space	splice
skid	slip	smash		spell	splint
skit	slow	smoke	**Grades 2/3**	spelling	splinter
	sly		sniff	spend	
Grades 3/4		**Grades 3/4**	snoop	spent	**Grades 3/4**
skate	**Grades 2/3**	smart	snowball	spill	splatter
skill	slab	smog		spin	spleen
skin	slam	smooth	**Grades 3/4**	spoon	splotch
skirt	sleek	smug	sneakers		
skyscraper	slim		snooze		**Grades 4/5/6**
	slope	**Grades 4/5/6**	snore	**Grades 3/4**	splatter
Grades 4/5/6		smear	snout	spaceship	splendid
skateboard	**Grades 3/4**	smock	snug	spare	splendor
skeleton	slant	smokestack		spear	splurge
sketch	slave	smolder	**Grades 4/5/6**	speed	
skillet	sleet	smack	snack	spent	
skinny	slice	smuggler	snare	spider	
skull	slick		sneak	spoke	
skunk	sling		sneakers	sponge	
	slippers		sneeze	sport	
			snicker		
	Grades 4/5/6		snorkel	**Grades 4/5/6**	
	slavery			spade	
	sleeve			spaghetti	
	sleigh			spank	
	slept			spark	
	sliced			sparkle	
	slight			sparrow	
	slippery			speak	
	sloppy			special	
	slot			speech	
				spinach	
				spoil	
				spooky	

Initial consonants blends/digraphs

spr	st	str	sw	tr	tw
Grades 1/2	**Grades 2/3**	**Grades 2/3**	**Grades 1/2**	**Grades 1/2**	**Grades 1/2**
spray	star	street	swan	trap	twig
spring	start	strip	swap	tray	twin
	state	strong	swat	tree	
Grades 2/3	step		swim	try	**Grades 2/3**
sprain	still	**Grades 3/4**	swing		tweet
spread	sting	strain		**Grades 2/3**	twice
sprout	stood	strap	**Grades 2/3**	trace	twist
	stop	straw	swamp	track	
Grades 3/4	story	strawberry	sway	train	**Grades 3/4**
sprig			sweep	trash	twelve
sprinkle	**Grades 3/4**	**Grades**	sweet	treat	twenty
sprung	stack	**4/5/6**	swell	tribe	twine
	stain	straight	swept	trip	twirl
Grades	stairs	strand		true	
4/5/6	stamp	strange	**Grades 3/4**	truly	**Grades**
sprawl	stand	stray	sweat	trunk	**4/5/6**
spread	steak	streak	swift		twelfth
spree	steal	stream	swish	**Grades 3/4**	twentieth
spruce	steel	stretch	switch	trade	twilight
spry	steam	strict		trail	twinkle
	stem	strike	**Grades**	travel	twitch
	stick	string	**4/5/6**	trick	
squ	stone	stripe	swallow	tried	
Grades 3/4	store	struggle	swamp	trot	
squad	stormy		swarm	trust	
square	stump		sway	truth	
squash			sweat		
squawk	**Grades**		sweater	**Grades**	
squeak	**4/5/6**		swindle	**4/5/6**	
squeeze	stable		switch	tractor	
squid	stage		swollen	traffic	
squint	staple		sword	trapeze	
squirt	starve		sworn	triangle	
	statue			troop	
Grades	steer			trouble	
4/5/6	stork				
squabble	storm				
squall	student				
squat	studio				
squirm	study				
squirrel					

The Spelling List and Word Study Resource Book · Scholastic Professional Books

Digraphs (two letters that make one sound)

ch

Grades 1/2
bunch
chair
chase
chat
chill
chin
each
lunch
punch

Grades 2/3
chain
champ
charm
check
cheek
chick
child
chunk
churn
inch
reach

Grades 3/4
beach
bench
bleach
catch
chair
chalk
chance
charge
check
cheese
cherries
chicken

chief
chose
church
coach
couch
ditch
itch
much
patch
peach
porch
pitch
rich
witch

Grades 4/5/6
branches
catcher
chimney
chipmunk
grandchild
hatchet
inches
ketchup
mischief
purchase
scratch
teacher
watchful
watchman
which

sh

Grades 1/2
bush
cash
crash

dish
fish
mash
push
she
ship
shop
shot
shut
wish

Grades 2/3
ash
brush
crush
hush
push
rush
shake
shape
sharp
sheep
sheet
shelf
shell
shift
shiny
shoe
short
shout
show
shower
trash
wash

Grades 3/4
flesh
fresh

shade
shadow
shall
shoes
should
shrimp

Grades 4/5/6
ashamed
bashful
fashion
horseshoe
marshal
marshmallow
seashore
sunshine
washer
Washington
worship

ph

Grades 2/3
graph
phone
phoned
photo

Grades 3/4
biography
dolphin
elephant
orphan
phonics
phrase
telephone
trophy

Grades 4/5/6
alphabet
atmosphere
cellophane
emphasis
emphasize
geography
gopher
megaphone
metaphor
nephew
pamphlet
paragraph
phantom
pharmacist
pharmacy
Pharoah
phase
pheasant
phenomenon
Phoenix
philosophy
phonebooth
phony
photo-finish
photograph
photography
physical
physician
physique
saxophone
symphony
triumphant

Digraphs (two letters that make one sound)

th ____

Grades 1/2
that
the
then
thin
this
with

Grades 2/3
bath
both
other
than
them
these

they
thing

Grades 3/4
birth
fourth
health
moth
nothing
teeth
thaw
their
think
thirty
throat

Grades 4/5/6
another
anything
depth
nothing
panther
thimble
thread
weather

wh ____

Grades 1/2
what
when
whip

white
why

Grades 2/3
whale
wheat
wheel
where
which
while

Grades 3/4
anywhere
nowhere
somewhere

whether
whine
whisper

Grades 4/5/6
afterwhile
elsewhere
somewhat
wharf
wheeze
whimper
whiskers
whistle
worthwhile

Long vowel sound of /y/

Long a
Grades 1/2
away
clay
day
gay
hay
may
May
pay
play
player
ray
say
stay
way

Grades 2/3
always
bay
birthday
bluejay
Friday
gray
maybe
Monday
playful
playground
playpen
Saturday
spray
Sunday
they
Thursday
today
tray
Tuesday
Wednesday

Grades 3/4
anyway
clay
delay

pray
stray
sway

Grades 4/5/6
balcony
betray
daytime
decay
delay
dismay
disobey
greyhound
holiday
Mayflower
mayor
obey
playwright
prey
survey
x-ray
yesterday

Long e
Grades 1/2
any
baby
body
bunny
candy
city
dolly
every
funny
happy
hurry
icy
lady
puppy
sandy
very

Grades 2/3
berry
buggy
daisy
donkey
easy
family
forty
hairy
jolly
lady
lucky
monkey
needy
only
party
penny
pretty
pony
rainy
rocky
silly
sleepy
snowy
story
very

Grades 3/4
activity
alley
already
anybody
anything
anyway
army
busy
drowsy
duty
empty
enemy
energy
fairy
fancy

February
fiery
fifty
filly
finally
eighty
hardly
heavy
holly
January
lovely
plenty
ready
really
somebody
storybook
storyteller
study
tardy
tiny
twenty

Grades 4/5/6
academy
actively
agency
assembly
battery
century
chimney
clumsy
country
deputy
documentary
dreary
eagerly
elementary
embassy
emergency
energy
extraordinary
faculty

fantasy
gravity
grocery
grouchy
heavy
jury
lonely
money
navy
nursery
quickly
sincerely
slippery
soupy
usually

Long i
Grades 1/2
by
cry
dry
fly
fry
my
sky
try
why

Grades 2/3
buy
eye
eyebrow
eyelash
firefly
goodbye
July
lullaby
myself
shy
sly
spy

Grades 3/4
butterfly
crying
dye
dyed
dying
lying
ply
pry
reply
spry
type

Grades 4/5/6
ally
analyze
apply
cycle
cyclone
defy
deny
dynamic
dynamite
encyclopedia
eyewitness
hyena
hygiene
multiply
notify
nylon
occupy
python
reply
rhyme
style
supply
typewriter

Doubling before ending

-ing

Grades 2/3

batting
begging
digging
getting
hopping
humming
napping
patting
planning
popping
putting
robbing
running
sagging
sitting
stepping
stopping
tapping
tugging

Grades 3/4

bragging
clapping
dragging
dropping
drumming
fitting
grabbing
grinning
hugging
rubbing
shopping
skinning
slugging
snapping
spotting
stepping
strapping

tagging
trapping
trimming
tripping
trotting
winning
wrapping
zipping

Grades 4/5/6

admitting
beginning
chatting
cramming
flipping
forgetting
hiccupping
jotting
kidding
knotting
matting
nabbing
nodding
plodding
plotting
prodding
quitting
shipping
shredding
skidding
skipping
snagging
stripping
submitting
swimming
throbbing
trimming
wrapping

-ed

Grades 2/3

batted
begged
chipped
dipped
dotted
fanned
flapped
flipped
hemmed
hopped
hugged
hummed
jammed
jogged
mapped
napped
nodded
patted
petted
pinned
planned
popped
rammed
ripped
robbed
rubbed
sagged
stepped
stopped
tapped
tugged

Grades 3/4

bragged
budded
capped
clapped
clipped

dragged
dripped
dropped
fitted
grabbed
grinned
hugged
matted
shopped
skinned
slammed
slugged
snapped
spotted
stepped
strapped
tagged
trapped
trimmed
tripped
trotted
wrapped
zipped

Grades 4/5/6

admitted
blabbed
chatted
crammed
equipped
hiccupped
jotted
kidded
knotted
matted
nabbed
nodded
occurred
omitted

patrolled
permitted
preferred
plodded
plotted
prodded
referred
regretted
shipped
shredded
skidded
skipped
snagged
stripped
submitted
throbbed
transferred
transmitted
trimmed

-er

Grades 2/3

batter
digger
dipper
hopper
jogger
logger
patter
planner
popper
robber
rubber
runner
sitter
stopper

Grades 3/4

bragger
clapper
dropper
drummer
fitter
hugger
shopper
slugger
snapper
winner
wrapper
zipper

Grades 4/5/6

babysitter
beginner
chatter
dinner
eyedropper
flapper
quitter
rapper
shredder
skipper
swimmer
trapper
transmitter
trimmer
trotter

Silent consonant patterns

kn

Grades 2/3
knew
know
knows
unknown

Grades 3/4
acknowledge
knee
kneel
knelt
knife
knight
knit
knitting
knock
knot
knowing
known

Grades 4/5/6
acknowledgment
knack
knapsack
knave
knead
knickerbocker
knickknack
knighthood
knives
knob
knocked
knocker
knockout
knoll
knothole
knotted
knotty
knowledge
knowledgeable
knuckle
penknife

wr

Grades 2/3
wrap
wreck
write
writer
written
wrote

Grades 3/4
wrapped
wrath
wreath
wren
wrench
wrestle
wrinkle
wrist
writing
wrong

Grades 4/5/6
awry
handwriting
overwrought
playwright
rewrite
shipwreck
typewriter
typewriting
unwrap
unwritten
wrack
wrangle
wrapper
wrapping
wreak
wreckage
wrestler
wretch
wretched
wriggle
wring

wringer
writ
writhe
wrongful
wrought
wrung
wry

gn

Grades 2/3
sign

Grades 3/4
assign
assigned
gnaw
reign
resign
sign

Grades 4/5/6
align
alignment
arraign
assignment
benign
bologna
campaign
champagne
Champaign
cologne
consign
consignment
deign
design
designer
ensign
feign
foreign
foreigner
gnarled
gnash

gnat
gnome
malign
signboard
sovereign
sovereignty

mb

Grades 2/3
climb
lamb

Grades 3/4
comb
dumb
limb
thumb
tomb

Grades 4/5/6
bomb
bomber
catacomb
climber
comber
crumb
honeycomb
lambskin
numb
plumb
plumber
plumbing
succumb
tombstone
womb

mn

Grades 3/4
autumn
column
condemn

solemn

Grades 4/5/6
hymn

bt

Grades 2/3
debt
doubt

Grades 3/4
doubtful
subtle

Grades 4/5/6
debtor
doubted
indebted
subtlety

lk

Grades 2/3
milk
talk
walk

Grades 3/4
chalk
folk
sidewalk
stalk

Grades 4/5/6
balk
caulk
folklore
folk tale
talkative
talker
walker
yolk

Long vowel in a silent letter pattern
(one or more letters is silent in a word where a vowel is long)

ai

Grades 1/2
mail
nail
pail
rail
sail
tail

Grades 2/3
afraid
gain
hail
main
paid
pain
paint
railroad
railway
rain
raised
sailboat
train

Grades 3/4
aid
aim
attain
await
bait
braid
brain
chain
claim
contain
dainty
detail
drain
entertain
fail
faint
gain
grain
jail

laid
maid
mainland
paid
painful
painter
rainbow
raindrop
rainfall
rainy
raisin
snail
stain
trail
trailer
waist
wait
waiter
waitress

Grades 4/5/6
abstain
acclaim
acquaint
acquaintance
ailment
appraisal
attainable
available
campaign
complain
complaint
container
daily
detain
drainage
entertainment
exclaim
explain
failure
faith
faithful
frail

gait
grail
hailstone
jailer
lair
maiden
maintain
maintenance
obtain
ordain
painstaking
praise
raider
remain
sailor
saint
sprain
stain
straight
sustain
waist

ea

Grades 1/2
deal
easy
eat
meal
pea
read
sea
tea

Grades 2/3
beach
bead
beak
beam
bean
beaver
clean
each
easily

jeans
lead
leak
leap
mean
meat
peach
peanut
plead
reader
reading
reason
scream
seat
speak
teach
teacher
team
weak
weaken

Grades 3/4
beast
beat
beaten
beneath
breathe
cheap
cheat
cleaner
creak
cream
creature
dream
dreamy
eager
eagle
east
eastern
feast
heat
heater
leader
leading

leaf
lean
least
leave
meantime
meanwhile
neat
northeast
peach
peak
pleasing
real
reasonable
repeat
reread
seam
season
seasonal
seaweed
sneak
southeast
speaker
squeak
squeal
steal
steam
stream
team
tease
treat
uneasy
weave
wheat

Grades 4/5/6
beacon
beast
bleach
bleacher
bleak
creamery
creamy
crease

daydream
decease
decrease
defeat
disease
downstream
easel
easygoing
eavesdrop
feature
flea
freak
freakish
greasy
heal
heap
heave
impeach
impeachment
increase
leaflet
leafy
league
lease
leash
leaving
moonbeam
piecemeal
reveal
seal
treason
treaty
weak
yeast
zeal

...Long vowel in a silent letter pattern

ei

Grades 2/3
either
neither

Grades 3/4
ceiling
field
leisure
receipt
seize

Grades 4/5/6
conceit
conceited
conceive
deceit
perceive
preconceive
receiver
seizure
sheik

igh

Grades 1/2
bright
fight
high
light
night
right
tight

Grades 2/3
delight
flight
fright
might
mighty
sight
tighten
tonight

Grades 3/4
brighten
daylight
delighted

eyesight
fighter
flashlight
frighten
frightful
headlight
midnight
lighten
lighter
nightfall
sign
sunlight
twilight
upright

Grades 4/5/6
airtight
almighty
candlelight
copyright
delightful
enlighten
knight
lighthouse
lightning
lighting
nightgown
nightmare
nighttime
outright
overnight
rightful
searchlight
slight
skylight
spotlight
starlight
thigh

oa

Grades 1/2
oak
oat

Grades 2/3
board
boat

coast
coat
goal
goat
groan
load
loan
moan
railroad
road
sailboat
toad
toast

Grades 3/4
aboard
boar
cloak
coach
coal
float
foam
foamy
loaf
loafer
oatmeal
roadside
roadway
roam
roast
soak
soap
toadstool
toaster
unload

Grades 4/5/6
afloat
approach
billboard
blackboard
bloat
boarder
boast
boastful
cardboard
coastal
coating

coax
flatboat
foal
groan
hoard
iceboat
hoax
lifeboat
loaves
moat
motorboat
overboard
overcoat
roach
seacoast
soapsuds
soapy
stagecoach
starboard
switchboard
throat
uproar

ow

Grades 1/2
blow
low
mow
owe
own
row
slow
snow
yellow

Grades 2/3
below
blower
bowl
crow
elbow
fellow
flow
follow
grow
hollow
know

lower
lowest
mower
owner
rowboat
show
slower
slowest
snowball
window

Grades 3/4
arrow
bowling
crowbar
flown
follow
grown
growth
knowing
known
meadow
ownership
pillow
shadow
shallow
shown
showy
snowflake
snowy
sorrow
sparrow
swallow
throw
widow

Grades 4/5/6
bellow
borrow
disown
lowland
marshmallow
minnow
narrow
outgrow
overflow
overgrown
overthrow

rainbow
scarecrow
sorrowful
stowaway
thrown
tomorrow
unknown
widower
willow

ue

Grades 1/2
blue
Sue

Grades 2/3
clue
due
value

Grades 3/4
avenue
continue
hue
rescue
statue
tissue
undue

Grades 4/5/6
barbecue
cue
discontinue
issue
pursue
residue
revenue
subdue
value
virtue

Complex vowel patterns

au

Grades 2/3

aunt
author
cause
haul
Paul

Grades 3/4

auburn
August
authorize
autograph
automatic
automobile
autumn
because
caught
caution
daughter
exhaust
faucet
fault
fauna
haunt
launch
laundry
precaution
sauce
saucer
sausage
taught

Grades 4/5/6

applaud
applause
assault
auction
audible
audience
auditorium
audio
aura
aurora
Australia
authentic
authority
autobiography
autocratic
autograph
automation
autonomous
autonomy
autopsy
autumnal
caucus
cauldron
cauliflower
cauterize
cautious
clause
default
exhaustion
faucet
faultless
faulty
flaunt
fraud
gaudy
gauntlet
gauze
Holocaust
hydraulic
inauguration
inexhaustible
leprechaun

maul
nausea
nauseate
nautical
nautilus
overhaul
paunch
pauper
pause
plausible
somersault
staunch
taunt
taut
thesaurus
trauma
traumatic
undaunted
vault

aw

Grades 2/3

draw
fawn
jaw
law
paw
raw
saw

Grades 3/4

awe
awful
awfully
awl
bawl
claw

crawfish
crawl
dawn
drawer
drawing
drawn
flaw
hawk
lawn
sawdust
sawmill
seesaw
straw
strawberry
thaw
yawn
withdraw

Grades 4/5/6

awesome
awkward
awning
brawl
brawn
brawny
dawdle
drawback
drawl
gawky
gnaw
guffaw
Hawthorn
jigsaw
lawbreaker
lawful
lawless
lawmaker
lawsuit

lawyer
pawn
prawn
scrawl
shawl
spawn
sprawl
squaw
squawk
tawdry
tawny
tomahawk
unlawful
withdrawal

ou

Grades 2/3

bought
brought

Grades 3/4

fought
ought
thought

Grades 4/5/6

afterthought
forethought
rethought
ought
overwrought
sought
thoughtful
thoughtless

The Spelling List and Word Study Resource Book · Scholastic Professional Books

Diphthong (the "sliding sound" made by two vowels)

oi

Grades 1/2
oil

Grades 2/3
boil
coil
coin
foil
join
soil
spoil
voice

Grades 3/4
broil
choice
joint
moist
noise
point
toil

Grades 4/5/6
appoint
avoid
ballpoint
checkpoint
disappoint
embroidery
endpoints
hoist
Illinois
invoice
loiter
moisture
noisier
noisy
ointment
poise
poison
recoil
rejoice
sirloin
tenderloin
toilet
turquoise
turmoil
void

ou

Grades 1/2
about
our
out

Grades 2/3
aloud
around
bound
cloud
count
flour
found
ground
hound
house
loud
mound
mouse
mouth
ouch
ounce
outer
outside
pound
round
sound
sour
wound

Grades 3/4
amount
blouse
bounce
cloudy
couch
doubt
foul
grouch
lighthouse
mount
mountain
noun
outdoors
outfit
outline
pouch
proud
scour
scout
shout
slouch
south

Grades 4/5/6
abound
account
aground
astound
background
battleground
bloodhound
campground
compound
crouch
devour
discount
drought
dumbfound
earthbound
foreground
foundation
fountain
gouge
greyhound
inbound
lounge
louse
newfound
ounce
outbound
outstanding
paramount
playground
profound
rebound
route
shroud
spouse
stout
tantamount
thundercloud
trousers
underground
voucher
warehouse

ow

Grades 1/2
bow-wow
brown
cow
down
how
meow
now
plow
town
wow

Grades 2/3
bowed
clown
crowd
crowned
meowed
owl
plowed
power
towel
tower
wowed

Grades 3/4
allow
clowned
crowned
flower
frown
frowned
Mayflower
howl
scowl

Grades 4/5/6
cauliflower
chowder
cower
drown
empower
fowl
overcrowd
overcrowded
overpower
powder
prowl
prowler
renowned
snowbound
superpower
vowed
vowel
willpower

oy

Grades 1/2
boy
joy
toy

Grades 2/3
cowboy
enjoy
royal

Grades 3/4
ahoy
annoy
boyhood
buoy
destroy
employ
enjoyment
joyful
joyous
loyal
joyous
ploy
soy

Grades 4/5/6
alloy
annoyance
boycott
boyish
clairvoyant
convoy
corduroy
coy
decoy
deploy
destroyer
disloyal
employer
employment
enjoyable
envoy
flamboyant
gargoyle
killjoy
loyalist
loyalty
oyster
royalist
royalty
viceroy
voyage

Prefix, suffix (a word part added to a root word)

un–
(Latin meaning "not")

Grades 2/3
unable
unbend
uncap
unclip
uncut
undo
unfit
unlock
unpack
unsafe
untie
unzip

Grades 3/4
unafraid
unaware
unblock
unborn
unbroken
unbutton
unchain
unchecked
unclean
unclear
unclosed
uncover
undone
undress
unearth
uneasy
uneven
unfair
unfelt
unfold
unfriendly
unglue
unhappy
unhook
unhurt

unkind
unknown
unlit
unload
unloved
unlucky
unpaid
unplug
unreal
unrest
unsafe
unseen
unsold
unsure
untrue
unusual
unwanted
unwind
unwise
unwrap

Grades 4/5/6
unaccustomed
unaffected
unanswered
unattractive
unaware
unbearable
unbecoming
unbelievable
uncertain
unchanged
uncharted
unclutter
uncombed
uncomfortable
uncommon
unconscious
uncrowded
undamaged
undecided
unequal
uneventful

unexpected
unexplored
unfamiliar
unfasten
unfinished
unfortunate
unfriendly
unhealthy
unidentified
unimaginable
unimportant
uninhabited
uninteresting
unlawful
unlikely
unmistakable
unnatural
unpleasant
unprotected
unravel
unreasonable
unrestrained
unsatisfactory
unscrew
unskilled
unspeakable
unsteady
unstopped
unsuccessful
untangle
unthinkable
untidy
untouched

re–
(Latin meaning "back" or "again")

Grades 2/3
react
redo
redraw

refill
reheat
remake
remove
renew
repay
reread
resell
reset
retake
retell
retie
retold
retry
return
reuse

Grades 3/4
rebound
rebuild
recall
recap
recheck
recopy
recover
recycle
rediscover
rejoin
relearn
reopen
repack
replace
report
rerun
reserve
restore
revise
rewash
rewind
rework
rewrap
rewrite

Grades 4/5/6
reapply
reappear
rearrange
reassure
reattach
rebuild
reclaim
recoil
recount
recover
reforest
reform
refuel
refuse
regain
regroup
rehearse
reinvest
release
renamed
repaid
repave
repent
replenish
repossess
reprieve
reproduce
republish
request
reserve
resolve
respond
restate
restoration
resume
retired
retrace
reunite
revealed
reverse
revision
rewritten

...Prefix, suffix

pre-
(Latin meaning "before" or "prior to")

Grades 2/3
precut
prefix
premix
preplan
preschool
pretest
prevent
preview

Grades 3/4
precook
predawn
predict
preflight
pregame
preheat
preorder
prepaid
prepare
presale
preshrunk

Grades 4/5/6
preamble
prearrange
precaution
precede
predetermine
prediction
predominate
preface
prehistoric
prejudge
prelude
premature
premeasure
premier
preoccupy

prepackage
preprimer
prequalify
prerinse
prescribe
prescription
preseason
preservation
preserve
preside
presumption
preteen
pretend
pretrial
prevail

sub-
(Latin meaning "under," "near" or "further")

Grades 3/4
subdue
submit
subway

Grades 4/5/6
subclass
subconscious
subdivide
subgroup
subhead
subject
sublease
sublet
sublime
subliminal
submarine
submerge
submersible
subplot
subscribe
subscription

subside
subsist
subsistence
subsoil
substance
substandard
subterranean
subtitle
subtotal
subtrahend
subtropical
subvocal

semi-
(Latin meaning "half" or "partially")

Grades 4/5/6
semiautomatic
semicircle
semicolon
semidry
semifinal
semiflexible
semiformal
semimoist
semiprecious
semiprivate
semirigid
semisoft
semisolid
semisweet
semitrailer
semitropical
semiweekly

hemi–
(Greek, meaning "half")

hemisphere

mis-
(Old English meaning "wrongly," "badly," "not correct")

Grades 4/5/6
misadventure
misbehave
miscalculate
miscast
misconception
misconduct
misconnect
misconstrue
miscue
misdeed
misdiagnose
misdial
misdo
misfile
misfit
misfortune
misguide
mishap
misinform
misjudge
mislabel
mislead
mismatch
misnomer
misplace
misprint
mispronounce
misquote
misread
misrepresent
mistreat
misunderstand
misunderstood

dis-
(Latin meaning "not" or "to do the opposite")

Grades 3/4
disable
disaster
disagree
disappear
disband
discolor
discomfort
disconnect
discontinue
discount
discover
disease
disgrace
disgust
dishonest
disjoin
dislike
dismiss
disobey
disorder
disown
displace
distrust

Grades 4/5/6
disability
disadvantage
disagreeable
disagreed
disagreement
disappoint
disapprove
disarray
disbelief
discard
discharge
discontent
discord

discourage
discovery
disengage
disgraceful
dislodge
disobey
displease
dispute
distort
distract

tele-
(Greek meaning "far off" or "distant")

Grades 4/5/6
telecast
telecommuni-
    cation
telegram
telegraph
telepathic
telepathy
telephone
telephoto
telescope
telescopic
telethon
teletype
televise
television

-less
(Old English meaning "devoid," "false," "lack of")

Grades 3/4
careless
colorless
countless
endless

helpless
homeless
hopeless
joyless
nameless
sleepless
soundless
tasteless
timeless
useless

Grades 4/5/6
ageless
changeless
cordless
listless
painless
priceless
reckless
regardless
speechless
thoughtless
tireless
worthless

-ful
(Old English meaning "to be full")

Grades 3/4
careful
cheerful
colorful
hateful
helpful
hopeful
joyful
powerful
skillful
truthful
useful
wonderful

Grades 4/5/6
awful
bashful
dreadful
faithful
fearful
graceful
harmful
neglectful
painful
peaceful
pitiful
regretful
resentful
respectful
scornful
skillful
sorrowful
successful
tearful
thoughtful
wasteful
watchful
wrathful

-ness
(Old English meaning "state," "condition," "quality," "degree")

Grades 3/4
boldness
darkness
dampness
firmness
fullness
goodness
kindness
likeness
openness
sharpness
shyness

softness
wetness

Grades 4/5/6
blindness
carefulness
cautiousness
cleverness
darkness
eagerness
effectiveness
emptiness
gentleness
happiness
heaviness
liveliness
looseness
smoothness
tenderness
toughness

-ship
(Old English meaning "to shape")

Grades 3/4
friendship
hardship
leadership
ownership

Grades 4/5/6
authorship
citizenship
courtship
craftsmanship
fellowship
internship
partnership
workmanship

-able/-ible
(Latin meaning "capable" or "worthy of;" *—able* onto base words [*depend/ dependable*), *-ible* onto root words [*cred/credible*])

Grades 3/4
breakable
climbable
comfortable
enjoyable
learnable
liftable
livable
lovable
readable
spreadable
thinkable
useable

Grades 4/5/6
acceptable
adorable
agreeable
allowable
available
believable
changeable
charitable
combustible
comparable
controllable
credible
dependable
desirable
dispensable
divisible
durable
edible
excusable

...Prefix, suffix

favorable	laughable	perishable	remarkable	valuable
flexible	legible	permissible	sensible	visible
forcible	miserable	possible	stackable	
gullible	notable	predictable	terrible	
horrible	noticeable	presentable	uncontrollable	
invisible	observable	profitable	unreasonable	

Doubling consonant at syllable juncture
(where two syllables meet)

Grades 3/4	happen	running	appeal	immune
annoy	hidden	sadden	appear	intelligent
apple	kettle	saddest	appoint	lullaby
battle	kitten	shopping	appreciate	marriage
bottle	letter	silly	arrange	misspell
bubble	little	sitting	arrangement	occasion
butter	manner	sorry	assume	omitted
button	marry	suffix	attribute	opposite
cattle	matter	summer	beginning	parallel
common	merry	supper	brilliant	patrolled
daddy	middle	support	bullet	permitted
dazzle	mommy	thinner	bulletin	pollen
differ	muffin	tunnel	committee	pollute
difficult	muzzle	winner	commute	possess
dollar	paddle	worry	correspond	recommend
fellow	pebble		difference	regretting
flatter	pillow	**Grades 4/5/6**	difficulty	scatter
follow	pretty	accommodate	disappear	shallow
fossil	puppet	accumulate	essay	struggle
funny	puzzle	accurate	exaggerate	summit
gallon	rabbit	address	forgetting	terrific
giggle	rattle	admitting	forgotten	upsetting
gossip	rotten	ally	illustrate	

Consonant alternations—Grades 4/5/6
(consonant sounds that are altered or eliminated from root words)

aristocrat–aristocracy
bomb–bombard
condemn–condemnation
confident–confidence
conspire–conspiracy
critic–criticize
democrat–democracy

design–designation
divide–division
fiction–fictitious
inquire–inquisition
magic–magician
medic–medicinal
moist–moisten

muscle–muscular
music–musician
part–partial
resign–resignation
sign–signal
sign–signature

Vowel alternations—Grades 4/5/6
(vowel sounds that are altered or eliminated from root words)

admire–admiration
agile–agility
angel–angelic
aristocrat–aristocracy
aspire–aspiration
athlete–athletic
brave–bravado
clean–cleanse
combine–combination
comedy–comedian
compete–competition
compose–composition
confide–confidence
console–consolation
conspire–conspiracy
creep–crept
decide–decision
define–definition
design–designation
deal–dealt

deep–depth
democrat–democracy
disciple–discipline
divide–dividend
ecology–ecological
exclaim–exclamation
explain–explanation
finite–infinity
geometry–geometric
heal–health
impose–imposition
invite–invitation
keep–kept
knee–knelt
leap–leapt
major–majority
mean–meant
metal–metallic
nation–national
nature–natural

number–numerous
oppose–opposition
precede–precedent
prepare–preparation
preserve–preservation
proclaim–proclamation
produce–production
province–provincial
realize–realization
recognize–recognition
reduce–reduction
reveal–revelation
revise–revision
sleep–slept
televise–television
sweep–swept
volcano–volcanic
weep–wept

Assimilated prefix—Grades 4/5/6
(prefix with a spellng change when added to particular root words)

in-/-il/-im/-ir (not, into)

illegal	immortal	increase	inform
illegible	immune	indefinite	informal
illiterate	impolite	indent	inhale
illogical	import	independence	inject
illusion	inaccurate	indirect	insane
illustrate	inactive	induce	invisible
imbalance	inclined	infer	irrational
immediate	include	infinite	irregular
immense	incomplete	inflame	irreplaceable
immigrant	incorrect	inflexible	irresponsible

-tion Variations

-tion
(Latin meaning "act," "process" or "condition of" [most common ending])

Grades 3/4
action
addition
auction
fiction
fraction
friction
lotion
mention
motion
multiplication
nation

Grades 4/5/6
admiration
affection
ambition

application
attention
celebration
circulation
combination
composition
concentration
condition
conversation
cooperation
creation
description
direction
education
election
emotion
expectation
identification
illustration
imagination
instruction
invention
isolation

location
motion
observation
population
position
presentation
reaction
satisfaction
suggestion
transportation
vacation
vegetation

-sion
(Latin meaning "act," "process" or "condition of" [add to base words that end in d/de or s/se])

Grades 4/5/6
admission

collision
comprehension
confusion
conversion
corrosion
decision
discussion
division
expansion
explosion
expression
extension
elusion
impression
infusion
invasion
mansion
mission
pension
profession
provision
revision
television

tension
transfusion
version
vision

-cian
(Latin meaning "one that is of" or "belonging to" [words end in c or are occupations])

Grades 4/5/6
beautician
clinician
electrician
magician
musician
optician
physician
politician
technician

Plurals, past tense, comparatives, superlatives

–ies

Grades 3/4
kitties
ladies
parties
puppies

Grades 4/5/6
abilities
activities
agencies
armies
companies
factories
families
ferries
hobbies
industries
injuries
memories
mysteries
opportunities
properties
qualities
victories

–es

Grades 2/3
ashes
boxes
dishes
dresses
fixes

flashes
foxes
horses
houses
inches
lunches
mixes
washes
wishes

Grades 3/4
axes
benches
branches
brushes
bushes
classes
crashes
crosses
glasses
grasses
hisses
kisses
messes
passes
presses
pushes
rashes
taxes
tosses
waxes

Grades 4/5/6
annexes

blesses
blushes
chatterboxes
climaxes
coaxes
duplexes
flexes
guesses
gushes
hoaxes
lashes
leashes
marshes
meshes
perplexes
pickaxes
prefixes
reflexes
sexes
slashes
smashes
splashes
swishes
thrashes

–ed

Grades 2/3
called
fixed
hooked
hoped
hopped
liked

loved
patted

Grades 3/4
cashed
clashed
dashed
finished
lashed
paced
removed
smashed
spotted
stopped
tripped

Grades 4/5/6
accomplished
arched
blamed
compressed
cracked
deceased
depressed
distinguished
experienced
followed
grabbed
iced
practiced
pronounced
raised
scared
slammed

striped
unbalanced
unfinished
voiced

–er

Grades 2/3
bigger
finer
fitter
fuller
hitter
hotter
lesser
littler
madder
mixer
nicer
redder
sadder
safer
taller
washer

Grades 3/4
blower
braver
closer
cooler
dresser
fairer
flatter
louder

remover
richer
sadder
sender
shopper
thinner
wider
worker
writer

Grades 4/5/6
catcher
cleaner
discoverer
follower
fresher
gunner
lover
murderer
server
sharper
speaker
spreader

stranger
talker
thicker

–ier

Grades 3/4
bloodier
busier
crazier
creepier
curlier
earlier
easier
flakier
funnier
happier
heavier
luckier
rainier
sillier
stickier

Grades 4/5/6
chubbier
clumsier
fancier
glossier
lonelier
moodier
nastier
noisier
prettier
shakier
steadier
stinkier
unluckier

–est

Grades 2/3
biggest
fattest
finest
hottest
littlest

nicest
reddest

Grades 3/4
closest
saddest
thinnest
widest

–iest

Grades 3/4
bloodiest
busiest
craziest
creepiest
curliest
earliest
easiest
flakiest
funniest
happiest
heaviest

luckiest
rainiest
silliest
stickiest

Grades 4/5/6
chubbiest
clumsiest
fanciest
glossiest
loneliest
moodiest
nastiest
noisiest
prettiest
shakiest
steadiest
unluckiest

Compound words

Grades 2/3
airplane
anybody
anyone
anyplace
anything
anywhere
baseball
bedroom
birthday
bluebird
bookbag
breakfast
campfire
cannot
cookbook
daylight
daytime
doghouse
football
grandfather
grandmother
hilltop
indoor
inside
into
nobody
noontime
outdoor
outside
pancake
pigpen
raincoat
sailboat
seesaw

somebody
someday
somehow
someone
something
sometime
somewhere
sunlight
sunshine
suntan
without

Grades 3/4
afternoon
always
background
bookcase
cardboard
downstairs
drugstore
earring
earthquake
everybody
everything
everywhere
fireplace
folktale
footprint
forever
grandparent
hamburger
handsome
himself
homesick
horseback

meanwhile
necklace
newscast
newspaper
overcome
railroad
rainbow
shoelace
shoreline
starfish
underwater
waterfall
whenever
wholesale
windshield
wristwatch

Grades 4/5/6
automobile
barefoot
basketball
birthplace
chalkboard
cheerleader
classmate
dugout
farewell
fingernail
firecracker
fireproof
flashlight
footsteps
forehead
grandchildren
grandstand

grapefruit
greenhouse
haircut
headache
heavyweight
highway
homemade
household
housework
iceberg
livestock
masterpiece
network
nevertheless
salesperson
skyscraper
smallpox
teammate
Thanksgiving
toothbrush
toothpaste
toothpick
touchdown
turnpike
sweetheart
underground
uproar
wheelchair
whereabouts
woodchuck
woodland
worthwhile

The Spelling List and Word Study Resource Book · Scholastic Professional Books

Homonyms
(words with the same sound but different meanings and spellings)

Grades 1/2
be, bee
blue, blew
buy, by
eye, I
no, know
one, won
read, red
sea, see
to, too, two
write, right

Grades 2/3
bear, bare
been, bin
by, buy, bye
days, daze
ewe, you
flower, flour
made, maid
mail, male
merry, marry, Mary
pale, pail
plane, plain
read, reed
rode, road
sail, sale
sew, so, sow
some, sum
tail, tale
toe, tow
way, weigh

Grades 3/4
ant, aunt
beat, beet
cent, sent, scent

fare, fair
hair, hare
hear, here
heard, herd
hour, our
its, it's
jeans, genes
lead, led
knead, need
knew, new
knot, not
main, mane
pair, pare, pear
pore, pour
sight, cite, site
stare, stair
sun, son
threw, through
their, there, they're
time, thyme
wait, weight
where, wear
weave, we've
wring, ring

Grades 4/5/6
aid, aide
cord, chord
creek, creak
die, dye
dough, doe
due, dew, do
earn, urn
flare, flair
fourth, forth
flea, flee
fur, fir

gate, gait
grate, great
Greece, grease
hay, hey
Jim, gym
haul, hall
heal, heel
laid, layed
lie, lye
Maine, mane, main
manner, manor
medal, meddle
mist, missed
pain, pane
past, passed
peace, piece
peer, pier
petal, pedal, peddle
pole, poll
pore, pour, poor
pray, prey
rote, wrote
rough, ruff
seen, scene
shoo, shoe
soar, sore
steak, stake
steel, steal
straight, strait
sweet, suite
symbol, cymbal
waist, waste
who's, whose
worn, warn
vale, veil
vane, vain, vein

Conclusion:
Memoirs of Two Word Lovers

Do you really think about words? —Jim Wheaton

All the time? —Hank Fresch

At a recent dinner together we entertained our husbands with some of the stories from this book. They posed the above questions and we simultaneously responded, "Yes, of course!" We weren't always such word lovers. Our own children's and students' questions about words sparked our interest. For, as we began to conduct research on how to improve spelling instruction we discovered that the stories behind words often explained why they are spelled as they are. We began to collect these fascinating tales. In time, our students, families, and others began to share their word stories with us as well.

For example, Mary Jo's mother found a story in her church bulletin about the origin of "scapegoat." In the ancient Jewish religion, the high priest would begin a purification ceremony by symbolically placing the sins of the assembled people onto the back of a goat. The goat would be driven out of the sanctuary, into the wilderness and, ultimately, to its death. That symbolic act gave us a modern-day word. Mary Jo's mother had not only saved the bulletin, but also added an arrow with the words "word study" next to it. Our fascination is infectious!

We all pause to select the just right word when speaking or writing. We rejoice with friends when new babies arrive, realizing the chosen name has special meaning. Proper names are words. And while this book is ending, the origin of names is a great place to start with your students' word history lessons.

If you become fascinated with words, we assure you, you will not become a "word nerd." Rather, you will become a storyteller. You will move students beyond the letters lined up to create a word and into the fascinating stories attached to them.

> *My words fly up, my thoughts remain below:*
> *Words without thoughts never to heaven go.*
> —William Shakespeare (1564–1616), *Hamlet*, Act 3 Scene 3

Resources

INTRODUCTION

Fresch, M.J. & Wheaton, A. (2002). *Teaching and Assessing Spelling: A practical approach that strikes the balance between whole-class and individualized instruction.* New York: Scholastic.

CHAPTER 1

Beal, G. (1992). *The Kingfisher Book of Words.* New York: Grisewood & Dempsey.

Bear, D.R., Invernizzi, M., Templeton, S. & Johnston, F. (2000). *Words Their Way: Word study for phonics, vocabulary, and spelling instruction.* Columbus, OH: Merrill.

Brook, D. (1998). *The Journey of English.* Illustrated by J.D. Zallinger. New York: Clarion.

Denning, K. & Leben, W. R. (1995). *English Vocabulary Elements.* New York: Oxford University Press.

Fifer, N. & Flowers, N. (1994). *Vocabulary from Classical Roots.* Cambridge, MA: Educators Publishing Service.

Gove. P.B. (Ed.). (1993). *Webster's Third New International Dictionary of the English Language Unabridged.* Springfield, MA: Merriam-Webster.

Grumei, W. (1961). *English Word Building from Latin and Greek.* Palo Alto, CA: Pacific Books.

Kennedy, J. (1996). *Word Stems: A dictionary.* New York: Soho Press.

Klausner, J. (1990). *Talk About English: How words travel and change.* New York: Crowell.

Thomas, L. & Tchudi, S. (1999). *A Brief History of the English Language.* Boston: Allyn and Bacon.

Traupman, J.C. (1995). *Latin & English Dictionary.* New York: Bantam.

Web sites

History of English
http://www.ruf.rice.edu/~kemmer/Words/chron.html

Vocabulary University
http://www.vocabulary.com/

CHAPTER 2

Almond, J. (1985). *Dictionary of Word Origins.* Secaucus, NJ: Citadel Press.

Branreth, G. (1988). *The Word Book.* London: Robson Books.

Bryson, B. (1990). *The Mother Tongue.* New York: William Morrow and Company.

Davies, P. (1981). *Roots: Family histories of familiar words.* New York: McGraw-Hill.

Feldman, G. & Feldman, P. (1994). *Acronym Soup: A stirring guide to our newest word form.* New York: William Morrow.

Flavell, L. & Flavell, R. (1992). *Dictionary of Idioms and Their Origins.* London: Kyle Cathie.

Fry, E.B., Kress, J.E., & Fountoukidis, D.L. (2000). *The Reading Teacher's Book of Lists* (4th ed.). Parramus, NJ: Prentice Hall.

Funk, W. (1950). *Word Origins.* New York: Wings Books.

Hoad, T.F. (1993). *The Concise Oxford Dictionary of English Etymology.* New York: Oxford University Press.

Jones, C. F. (1991). Illustrated by John O'Brien. *Mistakes That Worked.* NY: Doubleday.

Lederer, R. (1990). *Crazy English.* New York: Pocket Books.

Limburg, P. (1986). *Stories Behind Words.* New York: H.W. Wilson.

Merriam-Webster (1991). *The Merriam-Webster New Book of Word Histories.* Springfield, MA: Merriam-Webster.

Metcalf, A. (1999). *The World in so Many Words: A country-by-country tour of words that have shaped our language.* Boston: Houghton Mifflin.

Sarnoff, J. & Ruffins, R. (1981). *Words: A book about the origins of everyday words and phrases.* New York: Charles Scribner's Sons.

Shipley, J. (1945). *Dictionary of Word Origins.* New York: Dorset Press.

Vanoni, M. (1989). *Great Expressions: How our favorite words and phrases have come to mean what they mean.* New York: William Morrow.

Voorhees, D. (1993). *The Book of Totally Useless information.* New York: MJF books.

White, R. (1994). *An Avalanche of Anoraks.* New York: Crown Trade Paperbacks.

Web sites

Etymology: The science of word histories
http://www.geocities.com/SouthBeach/4195/words.htm

Interesting Word Histories
http://faculty.whatcom.ctc.edu/lthomp/personal/wordfor.htm

Word Play
http://www.wolinskyweb.net/word.htm

Ye Old English Sayings
http://www.rootsweb.com/~genepool/sayings.htm

CHAPTER 3

Flavell, L. & Flavell, R. (1992). *Dictionary of Idioms and Their Origins.* London: Kyle Cathie.

Flynn, N.T. (1988). *"Puttin' on the dog" A Potpourri of Colonial Sayings and Customs.* New York: Dover Publications.

Funk, C.E. (1993). *Heaven to Betsy & Other Curious Sayings.* New York: Harper Collins.

Hendrickson, R. (1997). *Facts on File of Word and Phrase Origin.* New York: Facts on File, Inc..

Mordock, J & Korach, M. (2001). *Common Phrases and Where They Come From.* New York: The Lyons Press.

Vanoni, M. (1989). *Great Expressions: How our favorite words and phrases have come to mean what they mean.* Illustrated by C. Demarest. New York: William Morrow.

Web sites

Activities for ESL Students
http://www.a4esl.org

Ancient Chinese Idioms
http://www.gis.net/~zhanghc/interests/idioms.html

English language practice
http://members.aol.com/eslkathy/esl.htm

Idioms/Figures of speech
http://www.essdack.org/tips/idiom.html

Map of idioms
http://www.geocities.com/FashionAvenue/Catwalk/4588/idioms.html

Toon in to Idioms http://www.elfs.com/2nN-1Xpix.html

CHAPTER 4

Blevins, W. (2001). *Teaching Phonics and Word Study in the Intermediate Grades.* New York: Scholastic.

Dale, E. & O'Rourke, J. (1976). *The Living Word Vocabulary.* Elgin, IL: Field Enterprises.

Fresch, M.J. & Wheaton, A. (2002). *Teaching and Assessing Spelling: A practical approach that strikes the balance between whole-class and individualized instruction.* New York: Scholastic.

Fry, E., Kress, J., & Fountoukidis. D. (2000). *The Reading Teacher's Book of Lists* (4th ed.). Englewood Cliffs, NJ: Prentice Hall.

Gove. P.B. (Ed.). (1993). *Webster's Third New International Dictionary of the English Language Unabridged.* Springfield, MA: Merriam-Webster.

Greene, H.A. (1961). *The New Iowa Spelling Scale.* Iowa City: State University of Iowa.

Hanna, P., Hanna, J, Hodges, R. & Rudorf, E. (1966). *Phoneme-grapheme Correspondences as Cues to Spelling Improvement.* Washington, D.C.: U.S. Department of Health, Education and Welfare.

Henderson, E. (1990). *Teaching Spelling* (2nd ed.). Boston: Houghton Mifflin.

Bolton, F. & Snowball, D. (1997). *Teaching Spelling: A practical resource.* Portsmouth, NH: Heinemann.

Stowe, C.M. (1996). *Spelling Smart!* West Nyack, NY: The Center for Applied Research in Education.